LIP SERVICE

BADASS

The Double Album

LIP SERVICE

BADASS

The Double Album

Published by Lominy Books
Davie, Florida
www.lominybooks.som

First Edition, November 2014
Copyright ©2014 Lominy Books

The views expressed in this book are those of the authors and do not necessarily reflect those of the publisher.

All rights reserved. This book, or parts thereof, may not be reproduced in any form without permission. The scanning, uploading, and distribution of this book via the Internet or via any other means without the permission of the publisher is illegal and punishable by law.

Please purchase only authorized editions, and do not participate in or encourage piracy of copyrighted materials. Your support of the authors' rights is appreciated.

Cover Artwork: "twin_s" by wendiwirawan ©2010
Cover Design: Charlotte Howard, CKH Design

ISBN-13: 0991082176
ISBN-10: 978-0-9910821-7-9

Printed in the United States of America

TABLE OF CONTENTS

7   The Second A-Side

13   Q&A with Andrea

15   Esther Martinez-Kenniff
        Born Again. Again.

25   Karen Sabine
        The Cat

35   R. David New
        How I Came to See It All Differently

45   Inessa Freylekhman
        Still Here

53   Daniel Jones
        Love, Illuminated

61   Cathi Hanauer
        First Things First

71   M.J. Fievre
        Cycle

81 Mary Rae Smith
    A Hairy Affair

THE SECOND A-SIDE

Thank you for flipping over (the book). Welcome to the second A-side. Please know that I don't consider the second A-side any less than the first A-side. It's just the other side of this double album. One side had to come first. And one side had to come second. Even though I know from history that some B-side hits got just as big or bigger than their A-side counterparts (it happened to both Elvis and The Beatles), this is not the B-side. It could be, but it's not. It's the other A-side, where you will get 8 more stories.

Hardly anyone ever asks me why we call ourselves Lip Service. Maybe they know the dictionary definition: *support for someone or something expressed in words but not actions*, which pretty much translates to: *talking shit*. I think they think, "Talking shit, yeah, I get it."

But what do they get? Giving lip service to something means talking shit. But our Lip Service is about truth. True stories.

I wish I could say I named the show or even that I'm smart enough to think of why Lip Service is a great name for a show about truth. But one of my friends in L.A. named it and at the time I thought, "Talking shit, yeah, I get it."

Then a few years ago, Esther and I were being interviewed on WLRN's Topical Currents. Joseph Cooper asked about the name and Esther said, "We're about truth, so it's funny, Joe. We're using the term Lip Service ironically."

I think it's fair to say I'm the beauty in this operation.

(Esther blonde, Andrea brunette)

Since you were good enough to buy this book, I thought I'd let you in on some of what we put into practice to create Lip Service. Over the last 8 years, we've learned that a story prepared for the stage is different than a story prepared for the page. For example, a story has to be simple to work on stage. Long descriptive passages, even beautiful ones, don't work. Nuanced literary stories don't work either. The audience is distracted. The audience gets tired. The audience only has one chance to hear the story. There is no flipping back to reread spaced-out-over lines. Stories have to be lean. Nothing extra.

We learned from WLRN, our local NPR station, when we did a show that aired on the radio, that what works best for stage and radio is one idea per sentence. So the sentence you just read, with multiple ideas (that WLRN is our local NPR station and that we did a show that aired on the radio and that we like one idea per sentence), would not work out loud. What works is a sentence like this: A sentence should have only one idea.

We also learned from WLRN that, when writing to the ear, a sentence, a paragraph, and even the whole story, should end on the strongest word or the main idea. This is especially important when dealing with a funny sentence or sequence of sentences because we don't want to bury the joke. For example, one time I told a story about testing my daughter for the gifted program, which was really a story about my own insecurity about my intelligence. Early in the story I mentioned that I'd gotten into the University of Pennsylvania not because I was a genius, but because I was a genius at tennis. These lines come later in the story:

I made sure we got plenty of rest the week before the (gifted) test. And drank tons of water to stay hydrated. The night before, we carbo-loaded on SpaghettiOs. I'm an athlete; I know how to prepare for competition.

Esther thought the funniest part was about the SpaghettiOs. So she thought the sequence should read:

I'm an athlete; I know how to prepare for competition. I made sure we got plenty of rest the week before the test. And drank tons of water to stay hydrated. The night before, we carbo-loaded on SpaghettiOs.

Esther is really good at hearing when a sentence or sentences should be inverted. I'm really good at trimming off the extra fat. For example: I'm good at trimming.

At Lip Service, we edit this hard, down to the micro level. A storyteller a few shows ago said, "You obsess over every word, but you don't have to." I'm not sure if that was a compliment.

Since this is a book, I tried to relax about the one-idea-per-sentence thing and some of the other Lip Service editing-for-the-ear techniques. But this has become my sensibility, so if I err on the side of simplicity, it's only because I can't help myself.

The stories for this anthology were picked based on several criteria, which are pretty much the same criteria we use to pick the stories for every show. We care about how the stories work together. We love it when stories talk to each other either content-wise, which happens when we present a theme and eight people approach it from their unique perspectives, or thematically, like "The Cat" and "Fake Murder." What these stories share is a confession without regret. (So refreshing.) "Obsessed," "Badass" and "Nitro & Glycerin" are identity stories. All three ask one of my favorite questions: Who am I?

We care about diversity, in terms of storytellers. We want a good mix of the population. We also care about diversity in terms of the tone of the stories. For example, all the stories can't be sad. We need breaks. And all the stories can't be funny for the same reason. The truth is, about 80% of the stories we receive are serious. So most of the stories we feature on stage are serious. This is probably why I can come out and say: "I got a 1090 on my SAT," and be bowled over by laughter. It helps if someone has just told a story about something very serious. Those stories help me seem a lot funnier than I probably am. Thank you, serious storytellers. But over all, what we care most about is a good story. Because more than anything, we want you to walk out feeling like you've connected with a total stranger, or 8 strangers. We want you to feel like I did the first time I saw the musical *Hair*. We want you to wave your arms in the air and sing, "Aquarius."

That said, these stories were hard to pick. Out of thirty-seven shows, over 8 years, I could have made thirty-seven books I'd be proud of. But that would have been way too many books. So I created another secret committee made up of people who are not as intimately connected to Lip Service and the storytellers (as Esther and I are) because it was impossible to judge these stories apart from the storytellers and the reactions they got from the live audience, and this is what the committee came up with for the second A-side. Enjoy!

Andrea Askowitz
Editor

Q&A WITH ANDREA
Editor

How does it feel to tell stories at Lip Service?
For the last 8 years, I have spent the two days before each show in the bathroom. I don't mean to be gross, but this is my body's physical response to how crazy nervous I get every single time. We've done thirty-seven shows, so that's seventy-four days—a lot of bathroom time. My mom's boyfriend, Bob, asked me why I do it, given my dislike for the bathroom. I do it because when I tell a story at Lip Service I feel like six hundred people understand me.

What do you do for work?
I write stories, teach writing classes, and produce Lip Service. I also take care of two kids and neglect one dog.

What do you do for fun?
I write stories, teach writing classes, and produce Lip Service. I also watch movies in bed with Victoria and admire my children while they're sleeping. I don't have fun doing anything else.

What is your dream job?
I'm working my dream job now. But since this is a dream, I'll take a Pulitzer Prize for Humor (a category

in need of creation) and a call from a *New Yorker* editor asking me to be a regular contributor.

Describe yourself in three words:
Based on my answers above: Boring. Predictable. Homebody.

How would someone else describe you?
Sex goddess. Isn't it obvious?

Tell us something your mother doesn't know.
My mom accuses me of using her as a salve for my conscience. Whenever I did anything wrong, like skip school, smoke pot, get so drunk I lost my underwear at Gator Growl, all I had to do was tell my mom on me and release my burden. She knows everything. I hope she knows how much I appreciate her. What a load off.

What actors/actresses do you have crushes on?
Susan Sarandon, purely for her looks. Jack Black for his everything.

What advice would you give your twenty-year-old self?
Saving the world is a noble pursuit, but kind of a waste of time. You can only really save yourself.

Where do you want to be in ten years?
Spain.

ESTHER MARTINEZ-KENNIFF
Born Again. Again.

Esther is the co-producer, editor, and director of Lip Service. She has a BA in literature writing from Columbia University and is completing her MFA in non-fiction at Florida International University, where she taught Writing & Rhetoric. Her work has appeared in the *Columbia Observer*, *Newsday*, *The Daily Beast*, *Sliver of Stone* and others. She lives in Miami with her husband, Sean, and their daughter, Lilou.

BORN AGAIN. AGAIN.
Esther Martinez-Kenniff

The baptismal pool at First Baptist Church of Fort Lauderdale is the size of a large Jacuzzi but without the bubbles. I stepped down into it where Pastor Jeremy was waiting. We were both wearing floor length baptismal gowns, like choir robes. Mine was pure white. We faced the crowd. There were about two thousand members that day—typical for a Sunday—and as I scanned the pews, I felt grateful. Grateful to have found my faith. Grateful that the pool was heated.

I'd been there before. Not in that pool, but at that moment, in that ritual, which was supposed to change my life forever. I was about to be born again. Again.

Sixteen years earlier, when I was sixteen, most of my peers were experimenting with normal things, like drugs and sex. Me? I was experimenting with the Holy Spirit.

I hated my life, like most teens. But when I say my parents were crazy, I don't mean they were overbearing. I mean, when my mother grounded me, she kept me home. From school. I mean, there was a daily fight in my house, which usually ended with a visit from the cops and my mother on the hood of the car, howling, and crying and begging my stepfather to stay. I mean, when I was finally allowed to have a boyfriend, he caught a fist in the face protecting me from my stepfather.

Then the same boyfriend who'd acted as my only protector—my first everything—dumped me for my best friend.

My mother, who was grieving her own break-up, said we needed a new start. We moved from Miami Beach to a house in Opa Locka, the Compton of South Florida. The house had metal bars on the windows.

My mother and my stepfather divorced. Then remarried. Each other.

My older sister turned eighteen and moved out.

I felt entirely alone. And, I had acne.

I started skipping school and spent afternoons hiding out in the park, listening to Depeche Mode on my Discman. I wore dark eyeliner, short skirts, and black army boots—imitation Doc Martens. I gave myself a tattoo with India ink stolen from Woolworth's. When that failed to get my mother's attention, I pierced my own nose with a sewing needle.

My mother said I needed Jesus.

She dragged me to a Pentecostal church. She said if I knew what was good for me I wouldn't put up a fight. I didn't.

The Church of New Life was on the second floor of a strip mall in Hialeah. We didn't exactly fit in. The women of New Life were humble and soft-spoken and didn't wear make-up or nail polish. The pastor was a sweet woman who reminded me of the fairy godmother from Cinderella—stout, with gray hair, naturally pink cheeks and pillowy arms. The first time she hugged me, I trusted her.

The service was pretty unremarkable. Simple worship songs followed by a reading of some passage from the Gospel of Luke. But then, during the closing prayer, Pastor Isabel began calling on the Holy Spirit. Everyone closed their eyes. All around me, the congregation stood with heads bowed, whispering prayers. I kept my eyes open.

The pastor's pleas grew louder. Occasionally, a congregant yelled out, "Alleluia." The whispering intensified until it felt like a wind blowing through that small room. Then the pastor's words lost their shape and she began crying out:

"Sarrrrebedeek baHo harrrakashkoo lu kunda laria keshke tookoo lel sala meshkHo kool sarrre."

I was scared.

Women who'd been meek and mild before the service started to shake and shout. One of them fainted. And the whole room erupted with this strange babbling.

My mother peeled one eye open, leaned into me, and whispered, "They're speaking in tongues."

If there's a language in heaven, shouldn't it be Dante's Italian? Now *that* is a beautiful language. Glossolalia—the term for speaking in tongues—is not pretty. The words—if you can call them words—are all "er's." And phlegm sounds.

So *why* did it move me?

Because I sensed there was something primitive taking place. Something that was being communicated to my soul, even if my brain didn't recognize the sounds. Because I trusted Pastor Isabel. Because I needed to believe in transformation. Because I needed to believe.

After the service, Pastor Isabel and I sat together for a long time. She asked me about my life. I told her how I felt abandoned by my father. Neglected by my mother. Unloved and misunderstood and entirely empty. She listened.

Then Pastor Isabel told *me* a story. She said Jesus's disciples were in the Upper Room, during the Pentecost—the holiday, which celebrates God giving the Torah to the Israelites. They were praying for the Holy Spirit when, suddenly, and this she read right out of the Bible, "A sound like the blowing of a violent wind came from heaven, and filled the whole house where they were sitting. All of them were filled with the Holy Spirit and began to speak in other tongues."

I became obsessed with this story. Every chance I got, I knelt and prayed for the Holy Spirit.

Nothing happened.

Pastor Isabel said God would grant any petition made by a pure heart. I thought I needed to purify myself. So I signed up for baptism classes, memorized my verses and, four weeks later, stood on the shore of a public beach wearing a white robe.

Thirty yards away, Pastor Isabel was waist-deep in the water. I walked toward her. The shore was rocky under my feet. The water, ice cold. To still myself, I imagined John the Baptist waiting for me in the River Jordan, where he would support my body as I faced the heavens before being submerged. I'd spend an eternal second beneath the surface, buried with Christ. Then I'd emerge. Resurrected. A new creation. And there would be the Holy Spirit, hovering over my head in the form of a white dove. And heavenly trumpets would blast. And angels would sing.

And all my acne would be gone.

Pastor Isabel interrupted my fantasy. She dipped me back before I was able to pinch my nose shut. Salt water rushed into my nostrils and eyes and I forgot to pray for the Holy Spirit, and before I realized this, I was out of the water, and people on the shore were clapping and shouting.

Pastor Isabel looked at me and smiled.

I scanned myself for Holy Spiritedness. I wanted to say something inspired. Something in tongues.

All I could think of was Lionel Richie's "All Night Long." "Tam bo li de say de moi ya. Hey Jambo Jumbo!"

I didn't say anything.

The Church of New Life had failed to deliver on its name. Shortly after my baptism, I stopped attending.

Two years ago, I joined a Baptist church. I was in a similar place as the sixteen-year-old me. I didn't live with my mom anymore, but the man I thought I would marry dumped me. They say God loves a broken spirit. Maybe He also loves a broken heart.

Again, I needed a new start. I signed up for another round of baptism classes.

The difference is, this last time, when I looked at the baptismal waters, I didn't expect miraculous transformation. I knew the only change that would result from my baptism was the change I was committing to make within myself.

Before my second baptism, I thought of Pastor Isabel who, in a strange way, put a promise in my heart. I don't believe in speaking in tongues. I think it's crazy. But I believe, whole-heartedly, that she believed in it. I believed in her. And in this world, without proof of anything supernatural, isn't the real magic that any of us manage to believe at all?

Pastor Jeremy placed a hand on my shoulder. We prayed. He dipped me back. This time, I remembered to pinch my nose.

Q&A WITH ESTHER
Author of "Born Again. Again."

How did it feel to tell this story at Lip Service?
It's funny, because as open as I am about all the ugly stuff in my life, I'm pretty protective of my faith, so I tend not to write much about it. I felt more vulnerable sharing this story than I have sharing stories about my dysfunctional childhood. I worried then (and still do now) that people might think I'm poking fun at the beliefs or rituals in my piece, when actually, I hope I am making them more rational.

What do you do for work?
I'm lucky. I run a real estate office and have such amazing hours I can also run a household. Being a mom gives me so much joy, I hate to call it work, but it's really more work than a full day at the office. Still, I wouldn't trade it for the world.

What do you do for fun?
The most fun thing I ever do is travel. I would gladly be poor my whole life if it meant taking fabulous vacations on a regular basis. I'm not in love with things, but I do love experiences.

What is your dream job?
Whatever it is, it wouldn't be a "job."

Describe yourself in three words:
Smart. Witty. Practical.

How would someone else describe you?
My husband says: beautiful, brilliant and loving. That's why I married him.

Tell us something your mother doesn't know.
She hardly knows me at all, and I'm safer that way.

What actors/actresses do you have crushes on?
I don't really have an actor/actress crush, but I am super hot for the Spanish national football team.

What advice would you give your sixteen-year-old self?
I wouldn't really give her any advice because I know she wouldn't take it. I'd probably just give her a hug and tell her everything was going to be okay—better than okay. Because it is.

Where do you want to be in ten years?
I just want to be happy. What that means has changed for me in the course of my life, so I can't say I know now what it will be in ten years, but I think as long as I have my sweet husband, my amazing children, and a little time to write, I'll be close.

KAREN SABINE
The Cat

Karen is a Midwesterner transplanted to San Francisco. She has two of the best and weirdest teenage sons on the planet and a cat named Abby, whom she loves with her whole heart.

THE CAT
Karen Sabine

It's 7:00 a.m. I'm in my pajamas in the kitchen, bent over the laptop. I Google: "Insulin. Overdose. Fatal." I scan the results, then add, "Cat."

"An insulin overdose can cause life-threatening hypoglycemia. A severe hypoglycemic shock will quickly lead to coma, which may be fatal if not immediately treated."

There's advice on how to avoid an insulin overdose, but I find nothing that specifies how much is fatal.

I hear my sons getting up so I close the laptop. I kiss their sleep-sweaty heads as they bounce into the kitchen. Ben is five and fully a boy now, but Nate, at three, still has his delicious baby scent.

While I rummage in the pantry for the oatmeal, the cat creeps into the kitchen and positions himself between my feet. My sons start up their usual clamor for Froot Loops. I look at them, then down at the yowling cat, and put the oatmeal back.

Ben finishes his cereal and the cat yowls for the leftover milk. I put the bowl on the floor. "But Mom," Ben says, "you said that cereal milk was bad for his diabetes."

Caught.

"I know, honey, but—" I sigh, reaching out with my toes to rub the cat's neck. "It's okay this once."

It's 10:00 p.m. My husband is still at work. Or somewhere. Bob hasn't been home before midnight in a long time. My sons are asleep. I'm back in the kitchen, getting a plate of leftover chicken from the refrigerator. The cat is winding himself around my ankles, bleating like a sheep. It is unquestionably a complaint. I unwrap the plate and put it on the floor. He sniffs at it.

"Go on," I say.

He takes a tiny lick, then sits back on his haunches and starts meowing at me again.

"Christ," I sigh, dumping the chicken into the garbage. I bring the glass vial and the syringe into my bedroom, knowing the cat will be on my heels. I sit cross-legged on the bed and he leaps up next to me, stiff and awkward. He lies down alongside me, pressing up as close as he can. I wonder if he notices that for once I'm not shoving him away.

I've been administering his injections long enough that I handle it like an army medic, or a drug addict, yanking off the protective cap with my teeth and filling it from the vial with one hand. He settles in and, accustomed to the procedure, does not pause in his purring as I push the plunger down and refill the syringe, over and over.

The cat was my husband's idea. I wanted a dog. But when we went to the animal shelter fifteen years ago—two newlyweds—this cat thrust both of its front paws through the bars of his cage, jamming its chin sideways against the metal in its effort to grab at us as we approached. When I gave it my fingers, it gripped them and licked at them like a dog until he was drooling. That was good enough for me.

Bob and I were both working eighteen-hour days at our respective law firms. We dragged ourselves through the door late at night, and the cat was instantly between ankles. He stood on his back feet and clutched at our pant legs with his front claws. I backed away, dodging his paws to save my clothes. Bob said I was heartless and scooped him up. But Bob was home even less than I was, and the cat was left wanting.

The cat was diabetic. He developed a perpetually leaky bladder, then leaky bowels. We had two sons by then, and I spent my days and nights feeding and cleaning three needy bodies. While I was biologically programmed to love my children despite any amount of literal or figurative shit, the same could not be said for the cat. Yet, I took him to the vet every two weeks. I drove across town to get his prescription food. I gave him insulin twice a day. But if he brushed against me, I bristled. I resented every bit of attention the cat demanded and every bit that was carelessly lavished on him, by anyone. When my husband, lying on the couch with the cat asleep on his chest, asked me to get up and retrieve something so he wouldn't have to disturb the cat, I knew in my bones that I was capable of murder.

By the time our older son started kindergarten, Bob and I were so tightly packed with bitterness that we could barely speak. Whenever we sat at the small kitchen table, we couldn't look at each other. We hadn't touched in months. We were dry-eyed and exhausted.

We decided to divorce. I decided to kill the cat.

That the cat must die seemed to me a logical, and unavoidable, product of the circumstances. His diabetes had gotten worse, and his body was a collection of failures. It was absolutely clear to me, in a way that very little else was, that I could no longer care for the cat. This was altruism, saving him from neglect. This, unlike all the rest, was suffering I could prevent.

It's clear I've used enough insulin. Within a minute of the third injection, the cat is breathing heavily through his mouth. He lurches toward the edge of the bed, and I lift him down onto the floor. He creeps under the bed, and I sit back down on top of it. I get up, grab a towel, and bring in his water bowl. I listen for any sound from beneath me, but there's silence.

I wait for the horror at myself to emerge, but there is nothing. I turn on the TV. Conan O'Brien leans on an elbow across his desk from a grinning starlet.

The next morning, the boys crawl into our bed. Instead of the usual weekend sleep-in, I hustle them into the kitchen. After breakfast, Bob and the boys are gardening in the backyard. Bob calls in to me and asks me to bring the pruning shears from the garage. I step into the cool darkness, crowded with the accumulation of more than a decade: boxes of books, furniture that no longer had a place, wedding gifts with tags still attached, the infant swing waiting there in the dark for the third child who won't be coming.

And there is the cat, lying on the concrete floor. He's so clearly dead.

Now, two years later, my sons don't talk about the divorce. However, they do talk about the cat. How much they miss him. And how completely unfair and awful it is that he had to die. These discussions always happen in the car, inspired by some lost-love song on the radio. There is one song in particular we have on CD—"Lately" by Stevie Wonder. It's the fourth song in, and as the third song ends, I adjust my rearview mirror to see Ben behind me.

He's always prepared to meet my eyes, and I raise my eyebrows to ask, "You ready? Or should we skip it this time?" He takes a deep breath and gives a tiny nod, his eyes sliding away from mine in the mirror. The song begins and his face goes still, and when it ends he asks for it again.

I engage in this ritual mourning with them like a penitent. Notwithstanding my lack of religious faith, I understand the flagellant's conviction that pain is the route to absolution. "Can you play the song again, Mom?" Yes, yes, yes, yes. I do not know whether I am healing their wounds or salting them.

During a recent car ride, when the song is over, Ben asks me, "How much did you love the cat?" He pauses. "Did you love him with your whole heart?"

I press my lips together. I want desperately to lie. "No. I didn't. Not with my whole heart. Not like I love you."

"Did you use to? Like, before we were born?"

My heart pounds as I drive. "I don't know, honey. I think I liked the idea of having a pet, but I didn't really love him."

He's silent a while. "Well," he says, "*I* loved him."

Q&A WITH KAREN
Author of "The Cat"

How did it feel to tell your story?
Great, until I had to start speaking. Then it got rough.

What do you do for work?
These days almost every lawsuit requires the exchange of relevant information, which is all emails and attachments. However, most lawyers like to hide the juicy stuff in a mountain of data, trying to overwhelm their opponent. I used to be a lawyer, but now I leave the litigating to the alpha dogs and just sit in a quiet corner with my laptop and use electronic search tools to sort through email evidence.

What do you do for fun?
We have Philly cheesesteak Tuesdays, which are the BEST. I also like reading and trampolining, but not at the same time.

What is your dream job?
I want to be Andrea Askowitz when I grow up.

Tell us something your mother doesn't know.
That I think she did a fabulous job raising me, notwithstanding my many neuroses.

What actors/actresses do you have crushes on?
Helen Mirren (duh), Javier Bardem (grrr), and Emma Stone (the twenty-something I wish I'd been).

What advice would you give your twenty-year-old self?
You don't know as much as you think you do, and finding out is the fun part.

Where do you want to be in ten years?
Somewhere remote, driving an old pickup truck, with lots of dogs running loose all over the place. And a few goats, definitely.

R. DAVID NEW
How I Came to See It All Differently

David was born and raised in Philadelphia, PA. He studied art at the Mason Gross School of the Arts at Rutgers University, the Tyler School of Art, Temple University, the University of the Arts in Philadelphia, the Fashion Institute of Technology, The Art Institute of Fort Lauderdale, and Florida Atlantic University. An artist at heart, David worked in his family's furniture business while creating his own interior design firm, R. David New Interior Design.

After losing his sight in 2001, David became an advocate for people with disabilities. He is currently chairman of the Miami Beach Disability Access Committee and chief promoter of Ability Explosion®. He is president of Power Access Inc., Access Now Inc., and the Miami Beach Council of the Blind (an affiliate of the Florida Council and the American Council of the Blind). David is also the owner and operator of American Chair Exchange, an Internet specialty furniture company catering to homes and businesses, and Ballooniverse, specialty balloons for parties and events. David lives in Miami Beach, Florida.

36// Badass

HOW I CAME TO SEE IT ALL DIFFERENTLY
R. David New

I knew I was gay since I was a kid, but I was afraid to act on it. Acting on it would mean it was true. Still, every guy who was physically fit and who had good hair was a fantasy object. As a teenager, I'd see a man with his chiseled chest showing through a T-shirt and obsess about him when I was alone. In the middle of the night, when no one could see me, I'd drive to the public library to pick up a gay newspaper from the newspaper boxes outside. I'd call the 900 numbers in the back pages, just to talk to gay men.

It was 1987 and I was seventeen. AIDS was all over the news, not just my gay papers. I was afraid to be gay, not just because of the stigma, but because being gay meant dying of AIDS.

But then another seventeen-year-old-boy, who worked with me at the mall, invited me over. He had a beautiful body and perfect straight black hair.

We smoked a joint and he touched my leg. I got very excited.

It lasted less than a minute, then I pulled up my pants and ran out. I got into my Jeep. The top was off and it was raining. I drove home, freaking out, crying.

I didn't touch a man again until I was twenty-one. Because I was too afraid to be gay in my hometown, I moved to South Beach.

I went to the Paragon, a dance club in a huge old theater. The place was packed wall-to-wall with beautiful gay men. I was like, "Oh my God! Oh my God!" I had never seen so many gay men.

I was standing at the bar when I saw this guy. Dark brown hair. Tall. He saw me looking at him. He walked over. Dimples. He offered to buy me a drink.

I was ready. And so nervous.

The sex was good. But it wasn't even the sex itself. It was allowing myself the pleasure for the first time. I was free. It sounds cliché, but it was true; I was somewhere new and I was someone new. I was finally me.

We were together maybe a month and, when it ended, I went on a binge. All I wanted was to have the most sex and the best sex. I had two or three different partners every day, sometimes in a bathroom or in a parking lot. I became addicted.

The most thrilling part was the hunt. I'd see a guy. I'd see him see me.

I fooled myself into thinking I was careful. If my cuticles were cracked, I wouldn't do anything with that hand. If I flossed my teeth and my gums bled, I wouldn't have oral sex.

I was so afraid of AIDS, I couldn't even talk about it.

I assumed, like most gay men, that I was negative. And I assumed that if the guy I was with didn't bring it up, then he was negative too. I never got tested.

I was living in a suspended reality. All around me people were dying of AIDS. I was blind.

Then, in October of 2000, I was admitted into the hospital for a fever that could not be controlled. When the blood work came back, the doctors asked me if I wanted my parents to leave the room. I said no and then the diagnosis came.

I found out I had AIDS and came out to my parents at the same time. To complete the trifecta, it was also my dad's birthday.

Although I was told that if I were diligent about taking my medications, everything would be okay, three months later I was rushed to the E.R. with severe pain. After three spinal taps, I was diagnosed with spinal meningitis.

I developed a lesion on my spinal cord, which caused me to be paralyzed from the waist down. All of my basic systems began to fail. I lost my hearing.

As I lay in the hospital bed, I noticed that the room was getting darker every day, as if a shade were being pulled down over my eyes. In a matter of days, I was totally and irreversibly blind.

I was scared. But my only choices were fight or die. Sometimes, I didn't know which was worse.

After two years in the hospital, my parents brought me home. The doctors said I was terminal and suggested hospice care, but my parents wouldn't accept that.

Slowly I healed. It took six months to regain my hearing all the way and two years before I learned to walk again. I never regained my sight.

I lost what was most pleasurable to me: the beauty of a man and the moment I see a man see me.

A couple of years later, I heard about a guy who also went blind from AIDS. I contacted him by phone and, for a year, we talked every day for hours. He was still vital and confident. His voice was deep and sexy.

And we had this huge thing in common. Most people who go blind from AIDS ultimately die, because sight is the last system to go. But he and I lived. It was like we were in a secret club. He knew instinctively what I was thinking. He understood me, like no one ever had. For the first time, it didn't matter what he looked like. For the first time, I equated sex with love.

One day we planned to meet. I waited for him to tell me when he was coming, but he never called and I never heard from him again.

It's been twelve years since I got AIDS and went blind. Now I connect with men emotionally first and then get closer physically. If I feel a bald spot, crazy teeth or a weird body thing, it can turn me off, but I'm looking for something more.

I'm still afraid to have sex. Of course, I'm afraid of contracting other STDs. That would complicate things. But now I'm a person with disabilities. I'm afraid no one will love me because of them.

It's funny; I see myself as the seventeen-year-old me: afraid again, but for different reasons. Now I have my heart to protect.

Q&A WITH DAVID
Author of "How I Came to See It All Differently"

Describe yourself in three words:
Creative. Ambitious. Self-starter.

How would someone else describe you in three words?
Inspirational. Strong. Resilient.

What's your day job?
President of Everything.

What's your dream job?
Doing what I'm doing but having more employees.

What advice would you give your seventeen-year-old self?
If you don't figure it out, it will figure you out.

How did it feel to tell this story at Lip Service?
It was liberating and I'm so glad I had the opportunity to do it.

What actors/actresses do you have crushes on?
I don't have crushes on celebs because I don't really know any, but I have a thing for Dan Savage from the podcast "The Savage Lovecast."

Tell us something your mother doesn't know.
I tell my mom everything but she can't seem to remember that I don't like mint jelly.

Where do you want to be in ten years?
In love.

INESSA FREYLEKHMAN
Still Here

Inessa is a Feng Shui practitioner and psychologist. She is the Feng Shui Healer in Residence at Canyon Ranch Hotel and Spa in Miami Beach. When she's not busy Feng Shui'ing the world, she takes memoir-writing classes at Lip Service Institute, which is some of the best therapy she's ever had.

For more information about Inessa, please visit her at **www.fengshuifromtheheart.com**

STILL HERE
Inessa Freylekhman

I have two cold sores as big as dimes on my upper lip. They look like rhino horns. Thanks to these new beauty marks, Michael, my fiancé, gives me a nickname in honor of my Soviet upbringing: Russian Rhino. Because it's too painful to smile in the normal way, I redesign my laugh, molding my mouth into an O.

While we eat lunch, one of the cold sores turns into a scab and rips off. A piece of lip lands on top of my salmon and cucumber salad. Even though we're engaged, the relationship is less than a year old—too young for gross-out moments like this.

"Ouch," Michael says.

"There goes my sex appeal," I say. My lip is bleeding.

He says, "Leprosy is not such a bad thing."

Michael is my Jewish, raven-haired, white, African wonder. After we were matched on eHarmony, we did the long-distance thing for four months, fell in lust, then in love. When Michael proposed, I relocated from Seattle to Miami.

"So now that you've seen what's behind the cold sore, are we still getting married?" I smile, but the question isn't entirely in jest.

He says nothing, his golden eyes clueless.

"Hello? Would you please say something? Anything?"

I hear my mom's voice in her thick Russian accent in my head. "Stop ask stupid question. Michael nice boy. Let him be."

Michael works as a chief financial officer. His accounting goes way beyond his occupation. He's more than economical with his words. He's miserly.

He says, "Why don't you throw that thing away first? Then we can talk about it."

Not exactly the encouragement I'm looking for, but better than silence.

I'm not sure how long I'm standing by the garbage bin when Michael walks up to me.

He says, "Why are you staring into the trash? What's wrong?"

I say, "Nothing and everything."

I was already in a bad mood before the collapse of the cold sore. I miss my parents. I miss my friends. I've gained five pounds.

I had spent ten years in my last relationship and it had gone nowhere. By the time I met Michael, I was in my late thirties. I knew what I wanted, so when he proposed after four months, I thought: This is it.

But I'm feeling insecure. A few days before, while we were cuddling in bed, I said, "My vagina needs attention."

Michael said, "Stop talking about your vagina."

I heard my mom's voice again. "What wrong with you? Why you say this word: Vagina! So vulgar!

Man don't like woman who speak like this. Stop talk so much."

"But it's a part of me," I said. "Like my hair, eyelashes, and elbows. I'm not going to pretend it doesn't exist."

"Yes, I know," he said. "But you don't have to keep pointing it out. I know it's there."

Michael needs mystery to feel passion. I need transparency. When I asked him to explain what he meant by "mystery," he said, "If I told you, then it wouldn't be mysterious anymore."

I know what a cold sore means because I looked it up in one of my self-help books. It's a festering worry. I can't help but think: Is the eruption on my face a sign of the fear of rejection that's festering inside of me?

I finish my salad and say, "Honey, I'm taking myself under the covers."

Michael never knows what to do with me when I get this way.

I face-plant on our bed and slam the door behind me. Then I feel guilty and leave it a crack open. The comforter is so dreary, I want to scratch holes in it with my nails. Michael insists that it's green. But it's *grey*.

I'm a feng shui practitioner and I know that grey is the color of indecision. We need a lot of decisiveness to make it to the chuppah. He's forty-six, and I'm thirty-seven. This is the first time either of us has been engaged. And the first time he's ever lived with someone. I've tried balancing the grey with a red pillow, the color for action and passion, but we need more.

We're integrating lives, but it's taking longer than I imagined, and it's becoming harder to stay positive. I know that a year isn't a long time to spend in a relationship when you're twenty-two, but I'm not twenty-two. I want to get married. Michael, however, doesn't want to plan the wedding until we get more "solid" in the relationship.

I don't feel that we need to be more solid. I'm perfectly fine with the malleable state of our connection. It can take years to achieve stability in a relationship, and I don't have that long. Thanks to my mother, I'm constantly reminded that the clock is ticking. "Inessa, you not young girl anymore. You must go to doctor and make sure everything work down there!"

I'm scared of losing Michael. He's the first man that I actually want to wake up with day after day. I love the way he smells, his touch and sense of humor. He gives me stability. And except for the grey comforter, Michael has changed everything else for me. He's purchased a second nightstand after I insisted that having only one could hold his single status in place.

"Very bad feng shui," I said. "It's called the 'one-nightstand syndrome.'"

"But I've already found you," he said. "What difference does it make now?"

"Yes, I know. But don't you want to keep me?"

He gave me the master bathroom, while he uses the guest bath. He even hung burnt-orange curtains to protect our good energy from flying out the window.

An hour later, Michael comes into the bedroom. I'm done spinning like a dreidel. He lies down next to me, puts his hand on my heart, and smiles. He says, "My Russian Rhino. Stop picking on the scab. Let it be."

I stop picking.

Michael says, "You're beautiful. I love you."

He doesn't tell me that everything will work out, but maybe he doesn't need to.

He's still here.

Q&A WITH INESSA
Author of "Still Here"

How did it feel to tell this story at Lip Service?
I was a nervous wreck. I should've had that vodka shot after all.

What do you do for work?
I'm a Feng Shui practitioner and a spiritual psychologist. I love helping women and men bounce back from break ups, open their hearts to love, and attract the right relationship. Feng Shui and psychology are the tools I use to help people achieve their dreams. I facilitate workshops at Canyon Ranch Hotel and Spa on Miami Beach.

What do you do for fun?
I love to go on play dates to the movies, yummy dinners, yoga and personal-growth workshops with my wonderful friends.

What is your dream job?
I'd like to have a portable lifestyle doing what I already do and collecting residual income from my products, seminars and books.

Describe yourself in three words:
Loving, authentic, and funny.

How would someone else describe you?
Intuitive, generous, and gregarious.

Tell us something your mother doesn't know.
I have a fused relationship with my mom so it's very hard to hide things from her.

What actors/actresses do you have crushes on?
I don't have any at the moment. The last actor I had a crush on was Javier Barden—but only in his role in *Eat Pray Love*.

What advice would you give your twenty-year-old self?
It gets better. I promise.

Where do you want to be in ten years?
I want to be living in my villa in Spain with my soulful and sexy husband, raising healthy, gorgeous babies.

DANIEL JONES
Love, Illuminated

Daniel is the editor of the world-famous column "Modern Love" in the *New York Times*. He's the author of *Love Illuminated: Exploring Life's Most Mystifying Subject (with the Help of 50,000 Strangers)*, and the novel *After Lucy*. He is the editor of *Modern Love: 50 True and Extraordinary Tales of Desire, Deceit and Devotion* and *The Bastard on the Couch: 27 Men Try Really Hard to Explain Their Feelings About Love, Loss, Fatherhood and Freedom*. His writing has appeared in The *New York Times*, *Elle*, *Parade*, *Harper's Bazaar*, *Good Housekeeping*, *Real Simple*, and elsewhere. He is also the father of two children and the husband of writer Cathi Hanauer.

LOVE, ILLUMINATED
Daniel Jones

When Cathi and I met, she wasn't looking for someone like me. By "someone like me," I mean a passive underachiever with a subsistence-level income. Not that I didn't have positive qualities back then. It's just that ambition and earning power weren't among them.

We met more than two decades ago, before algorithms and online dating sites told us whom to love. I could have used some dating-compatibility assistance in those days. I had been struggling in love. Love scared me, especially its early phases where you had to risk rejection. I had neither the nerve nor the energy to put myself out there.

Then Cathi came to town—to Tucson, Arizona, where I was in the graduate writing program. Though we were the same age, twenty-seven, Cathi had spent her post-college years ascending editorial mastheads in the New York magazine world and was looking to attend graduate school as a way to slow down so she could write. I, on the other hand, had grabbed my college degree a year later than she did (having been held back in kindergarten) and, after graduating, headed west to Park City, Utah, where I found work as a ski instructor (winters only) and janitor (all seasons).

For two years, I skied and mopped. It was fun, but skiing and mopping have their limits. So two years later, eager for a fresh challenge, I decided to head to

Tucson to spend a few years learning how to write short stories. Many semesters later, with graduation looming and my future employment looking doubtful, I'd grown so lethargic that, by the time Cathi came to town, I was having trouble coming up with reasons to leave my room.

Which is exactly why we met.

True to her meticulous nature, Cathi researches all options before making any decision. So rather than rely on a phone call to get the inside scoop on Arizona's graduate writing program, she got her magazine to fly her across the country on assignment so she could check it out firsthand.

After meeting with the program director and probing him for all he had to offer, she asked for the names and numbers of female students who might be willing to share their perspective with her over lunch. She asked specifically for female students because she wanted to hear about a woman's experience in the graduate program.

Since I'm not a woman (and wasn't then either), I don't know why the program director added my name to the list he gave her. Whatever the reason, Cathi and I were destined to meet, because none of the women the director mentioned would have lunch with her. They were all much too busy. Whereas, when my phone rang on that fateful morning, I was sitting on my bed in a pre-coffee daze, watching my potted cactus grow.

Free lunch? You bet.

An hour later, over sandwiches and Cokes, Cathi, as the journalist she is, began peppering me with questions that were as much about me as the graduate program: "Where are you from? What do you write? Do you have siblings? Roommates?"

Still groggy, I struggled to respond to each one before she'd fire the next: "What's your favorite novel?"

"Um—," I said.

"What magazines do you read?"

"Oh, a lot of them," I stammered. "Most of them."

Cathi's final request was to see some writing from the program, so after lunch we strolled back to the English department. I grabbed a story of mine and handed it over.

The next week, I received a letter from her. (Yes, an actual posted letter from New York—this was 1989.) She thanked me for meeting with her and helping her out. She said she'd read my story in her bathtub and loved it. Later she would tell me her bathtub reading experience was when she first began falling for me. And I would confess that imagining her in a bathtub enjoying my writing was when I first began falling for her.

Soon, via letters, we tried to figure out if we might be right for each other. We seized on coincidences (like having been born only ten days and ten miles apart) as signs of romantic potential. Then Cathi applied to school in Tucson and was accepted. A few months later, I flew east to help her move. We made the trip in a Jeep we bought together (I picked it out; she paid) and began living in the same town. Eventually, we decided we were in love, the lifelong variety.

Within eighteen months of meeting, we were engaged and, less than a year after that, we married. She had to be the one to ask me, of course, but I swear I was totally on the verge of asking her.

Not long ago, as research for a book I was writing, Cathi and I signed up for several online dating sites. Along with learning how online dating worked, I wanted to see if we might have found each other that way. To explain our single status, I said I was divorced while she claimed to be widowed. Otherwise we answered all questions truthfully.

Unfortunately, none of the matches that soon filled our inboxes included each other. No matter how many times I hit "reload" or how far I scrolled, Cathi was never recommended for me, nor was I for her.

Why? Evidently she put her sought-after income at a much higher level than the modest amount I'd confessed to making. So, instead, she was directed to more "compatible" matches, like Leo, a divorced money-market manager with an income three times what I earn.

Is that why Cathi and I weren't recommended for each other—because of our incompatibility over income?

Yes. Leo was the guy for her. The only problem was Cathi didn't think she liked Leo, or any of the other "Leos" the sites kept feeding her. She liked me. Even though she *still* wasn't looking for "someone like me," I was the one she wanted—then and now. So much for the power of number crunching when it comes to determining compatibility.

Cathi was better off not setting her own parameters for love. She needed someone else to step in and add my name to her lunch list. Luckily for me, someone did.

Q&A WITH DANIEL
Author of "Love, Illuminated"

How did it feel to tell this story at Lip Service?
It felt warm, but not humid.

Describe yourself in three words:
I will describe myself with the three words a reviewer used—droll, compassionate, non-judgmental—and hope they are true.

Describe your wife in three words:
Energetic, exhausted, and gorgeous (of course!).

What's your day job?
I edit the "Modern Love" column in the *New York Times* and write a book every ten years.

What's your dream job?
Treehouse architect.

How would you define true love?
As I say in my book, *Love, Illuminated*, ET is the embodiment of true love: it's all about healing wounds and being good.

What is it like being married to someone in the same industry/line of work?
Great. It's like having an in-house editor for free.

What has editing the "Modern Love" column taught you?
That love is one of the few things our species can't seem to master or even get much better at from one generation to the next.

What actors/actresses do you have crushes on?
The only actress I've ever had a serious crush on was Jodie Foster, when I was twelve, and she was twelve too.

What advice would you give your pre-married self?
Love is more complicated than just being nice to each other—roll with it.

CATHI HANAUER
First Things First

Cathi is the *New York Times* bestselling author of three novels—*Gone, Sweet Ruin,* and *My Sister's Bones*—and the editor of the essay anthology *The Bitch in the House: 26 Women Tell the Truth about Sex, Solitude, Work, Motherhood and Marriage*. She has written for the *New York Times, Elle, O-The Oprah Magazine, Self, Real Simple, Whole Living,* and many other magazines. She was the monthly books columnist for both *Glamour* and *Mademoiselle* and wrote the monthly advice column "Relating" in *Seventeen* magazine for seven years. She lives in Massachusetts with her husband, writer and editor Daniel Jones, and their two children.

FIRST THINGS FIRST
Cathy Hanauer

First things first: Yes, I did put the ideal income on match.com a tiny bit higher than what Dan makes. Okay, a lot higher. But, listen, Dan put the ideal height for his match at five-foot-four, and I'm only five-three. Okay, five-two. Whatever, five-one. So that's probably why we weren't matched! And yet, here we are, happy husband and wife.

That leads to what I want to write about: being a wife. Lately I've been on tour with Dan for his new book. And even though we've been married for years, in some ways this feels like my first real experience as a "wife."

By "wife," I mean: the dutiful helpmate, the second fiddle, the lesser of two egos.

I was pronounced "wife" twenty-two years ago, but I never relished the label, or the position. Our marriage would be a *partnership*, I had decided. No traditional gender roles—though if I had to choose a role for myself, it would have been husband.

Being the husband suited me. As the oldest of four siblings, I was always the first, the boss, the center of attention. When Dan and I got married, I was making more money. I also was more ambitious. While I was clawing my way to the top, he was clawing his way through a Doritos bag. I published my first novel before he published his. He was generous and supportive about it, because, well, that's Dan. Plus, we needed the cash.

Dan, meanwhile, was the second-born in his family. His older brother actually talked for Dan until he was five, which, as you read earlier, led Dan to be held back in kindergarten.

So we were perfectly matched: I was his older brother, and he was my younger sisters.

After I published my first novel and Dan followed with his, I published an essay anthology—*The Bitch in the House*—and then he responded with his anthology, *The Bastard on the Couch*. They both did well, but mine became a *New York Times* bestseller. I was on the *Today Show* with Katie. I traveled around speaking before large audiences of women. (The book was about the stress of combining work with motherhood.) Dan cheered me on from home, where he was driving carpools, packing lunchboxes, and checking my Amazon.com sales rank to see how much we were making in royalties.

While having a best-selling book isn't exactly like being Beyoncé, *Bitch* did give me cachet, especially among literary sorts and Type A working mothers. I'd walk into my local bookstore and someone would yell, "The Bitch is in the House!"

At my kids' school events, people would say, "*You're* the one who did Bitch in the House!"

Dan would smile. "Yup! That's Cathi. She's that bitch."

It was good times.

But, then, things changed. While I was home writing my last two novels, I took over managing our children. Dan was editing a column in the *New York Times* called "Modern Love." Ten years ago, we were invited together to start the column. But, shortly into the work, we decided it was a better fit for Dan, since I was writing a book at the time and he was under employed.

Soon Dan built "Modern Love" into a phenomenon. Now, it's among the most read features in the entire Sunday *New York Times*. Dan's column has launched a few hundred writers and directly spawned thirty-nine books. People follow it religiously and are dying to write for it.

On Dan's tour, fans flock to meet him. They slip him their manuscripts. Women shriek, "Oh my GOD, you're the one who does Modern Love?"

I stand by, wondering, How did this happen? I pipe up: "I actually started the column with him!" But no one hears me. My words are dying bees.

Two weeks ago, we attended a book festival at the University of Arizona, where Dan and I went to graduate school. Dan was a featured speaker. He was flown in and put up in a glitzy resort. Though I've published the same number of books, I was "allowed" to come along as "Dan's wife."

At the opening reception, Dan wore the VIP pre-made plastic nametag. I got the white paper stick-on "wife" one. I could scribble in my name with a Sharpie, if anyone could bother to find one. A nationally syndicated advice columnist just around my age approached us, looked past me, and reached out to shake Dan's hand.

And I didn't blame her—really, I didn't. There's a sad dichotomy in this country between working women and stay-at-home mothers and wives—something I know because *I have written books about it!* I knew this woman figured I'd have nothing of interest to say to her, home in my presumed life of bake sales and mid-day Pilates classes. To let her know that I was hardly the typical Wife, I said, "I was an advice columnist too. I wrote the 'Relating' column in *Seventeen* magazine." I smiled humbly. "For seven years," I added.

"Really," she said. She scanned the room to find someone, *anyone*, more interesting.

"Yes," I yelled. "And I also—" I was going to tell her I had four books (she had two), and that one sold in sixteen countries. By then, however, she had slipped away to go freshen up her lipstick.

But, as the week in Arizona went on, a funny thing happened. Without kids to manhandle—they were now old enough to stay home and handle themselves—and without pressing work to do—because Dan now earns enough so that I can take on less—I began to relax into the role of The Wife.

In our room, Dan filed his column between doing radio interviews; I lounged in bed. Later, I went to the café and brought him up coffee and scones. At the pool, surrounded by toned women in expensive bikinis who sipped smoothies while their husbands huddled over laptops in the "business center," I thought, "I can do this."

After so many years of the power and prestige, yes, but also the stress and chaos of work and children, it was nice to be the one who got to chill out. When I told Dan, after that dinner in Arizona, that all night I'd felt like the wife, he said, "I spent a lot of years being the wife. It's your turn."

He was right. The poet Michael Blumenthal describes this phenomenon beautifully in his poem "A Marriage," which we happen to have read at our wedding:

You are holding up a ceiling [the poem goes]
with both arms. It is very heavy,
but you must hold it up, or else
it will fall down on you. Your arms
are tired, terribly tired,
and, as the day goes on, it feels
as if either your arms or the ceiling
will soon collapse.
But then,
unexpectedly,
something wonderful happens:

Someone,
a man or a woman,
walks into the room
and holds their arms up
to the ceiling beside you.
So you finally get
to take down your arms.
You feel the relief of respite,
the blood flowing back
to your fingers and arms.
And when your partner's arms tire,
you hold up your own
to relieve him again.
And it can go on like this
for many years
without the house falling.

    Thanks to Dan, it was, and *is,* my turn to let go of the ceiling for a while. He can hold it up—and be praised for doing so—while I sip a smoothie and slather on my sunscreen.

Q&A WITH CATHI
Author of "First Things First"

How did it feel to tell this story at Lip Service?
FUN! It was a blast to be on stage reading to a dark room and hearing people laugh.

Describe yourself in three words:
Tiny. Chatty. Manic.

Describe Dan in three words:
Calm. Wry. Smart.

What's your day job?
Writer, sometimes editor.

What's your dream job?
Writer, sometimes editor!

Tell us one thing you'd change about Dan.
I'd make him slightly more chivalrous—as he knows.

What would Dan change about you?
He'd have me talk less. A LOT less.

What actors/actresses do you have crushes on?
I don't get crushes on actors and actresses. Oh okay, Channing Tatum, Jeff Bridges, and Billy Crudup (in *Almost Famous*).

What advice would you give your pre-"wife" self?
Take everything you think you know about motherhood and disregard it. (It wasn't marriage that surprised me. It was becoming a mother.)

Where do you want to be in ten years?
Right about where I am now, except with more books published, more money, more job security, two kids done with college, and maybe some small way to "divide my time" (which has always been a goal).

M.J. FIEVRE
Cycle

M.J. obtained her MFA from the creative writing program at Florida International University. Her short stories and poems have appeared in *Haiti Noir*, *The Beautiful Anthology*, *The Mom Egg*, *The Southeast Review*, and *The Caribbean Writer*. M.J. is the founding editor of *Sliver of Stone Magazine*, and a regular contributor to *The Nervous Breakdown*. She is also a proud member of the Miami Poetry Collective. She's a Board Member of Women Writers of Haitian Descent, Inc., and edited the Haiti anthology *So Spoke the Earth*. She blogs at mjfievre.com.

CYCLE:
A Story in Four Parts about Bipolar Disorder
M.J. Fievre

I.

I'm looking at the teacher's carefully manicured hands as she clutches the Expo marker to write on the board. She's wearing a green suit—she tells her seventh-grade students that green is one of her favorite colors. Green and brown. Only she says *maroon* instead of brown. The teacher doesn't smile; she doesn't frown either.

I've been watching the teacher for months now. She arrives an hour before clock-in time, plans detailed lessons, writes comments on essays, allows soft chatter during group activities. When the principal stops by, he nods, impressed by her professional demeanor, the cleanliness of her classroom.

From time to time, I lose track of the teacher—I hear her voice in the background, talking about parts of speech.

"Ma'am?" a student asks. "What does auto-pilot mean?"

The teacher's mouth opens. The words stream out.

I want to relate to that woman in the green suit—but I feel so distant from her. All I can do is watch. Watch her manicured hands, *my* manicured hands. Her shiny shoes—*my* shiny shoes. I wonder: *Is she really me?*

There's a knock on the door. A student I don't know comes in with an envelope. "Are you the teacher?" she asks me.

"Yes," I say. "I'm Ms. Fievre."

She says she has a message for me. Then she says, "Nice suit."

I smile. "I love green. Green and maroon."

II.

Something simple happens. Maybe an invitation to a party. A phone call from an old friend. A picture from one of my students.

I feel alive.

Ideas are fast. I plan a party, make all the phone calls, frantically text message and email, pay for the VIP table out of my own pocket. My calendar is suddenly full—fashion show on Thursday, happy hour on Friday. A shopping spree is in order.

On the expressway, I hallucinate shadow people, colorful patterns, and spots. I can see outlines around moving objects.

At Sawgrass Mills Mall, my sister points at the pair of shoes I'm holding. "They're two hundred bucks, you know."

I giggle—not sure what's funny. My sister asks if I'm high.

"I'm naturally high," I say.

I do a jig in the middle of the store. I don't care that people stare.

I'm happy the whole week, cheer up my friends, mail an expensive gift to my little brother, leave witty notes on my coworker's desk. Danny says, "There's a positive aura, almost palpable, around you. You're so fun. We should hang out more often."

I've never been so productive, while others are wasting their time, sleeping. Clichés make sense: I'll sleep when I'm dead.

III.

I haven't slept for days.

Sleeping pills work—for an hour or two. Then I'm awake again, and sometimes I lose track of how many pills I've taken. There is no moon and the darkness is almost complete outside. I peer into the blackness, wishing I had the senses of a night creature.

Confusion replaces clarity. I'm sitting in front of the laptop, trying to remember my Hotmail password. That same password I've used for the past ten years.

My mind has burned out.

At work, I almost start crying when Julie asks me if I've gained weight. People are just mean and frightening. I feel ashamed.

"Ashamed of what?" my sister asks.

I say I have no idea. She hugs me, buys me lunch at J.P. Mulligan's, walks my dog, waters my desert roses. "It will get better," she says. "It always does."

I remember reading about some guy who stayed awake for 266 hours, just a little more than eleven days. I wonder how long I could live without sleep.

I remember reading about some guy from Dallas who led the police on a high-speed chase through two counties, ignoring the sirens and lights. He later said he was trying to get his dying cat to a vet. "What a guy," they said. "A hero." Then they found thirty-seven dead cats inside an old freezer, right beside the man's strawberry sherbet and chicken drumsticks.

At night, I'm sweating. My mouth is dry; my lips are tingling. *Maybe I'm dying. Or is this all in my head?* I'm not sure where my imagination ends and the cuckoo begins.

IV.

It does get better.

I've been weighed down for days by the cuckoo that lives inside me, that always seems separate from the me that walks and sees and remembers and forgets. The cuckoo crushes my belief system, my faith—but it doesn't last.

It never lasts.

The teacher comes back, manicured hands, high-heeled shoes, green suit.

Her image stares back in the mirror. I am completely captivated. *Is that really me?* I want so desperately to make that woman feel safe. But every time I reach, my hand only meets the glass she is stuck behind.

The teacher calls Danny, tells him she was drunk that night when she flirted with him—she just doesn't mention that she was naturally drunk. The teacher talks to Julie. *Yes, I've gained weight. I didn't mean to call you a bitch.*

The teacher talks calmly. She's matter-of-fact.

And I'm there again, watching.

Q&A WITH M.J.
Author of "Cycle"

How did it feel to tell this story at Lip Service?
At first, the idea was nerve-wracking. I grew up in Haiti, in a society that teaches that it's absolutely not okay to air one's dirty laundry. My piece was really personal and, although I'm committed to nonfiction, I prefer to hide behind a computer screen. When I'm nervous, my accent gets very thick and the muscles in my jaw clench and unclench. My hands tremble, and I have to remember not to knot them behind my back. I'm a writer, not a performer. So, I'm glad Andrea and Esther held a rehearsal in a house full of cheery warmth. I was able to get over the stage fright. Somewhat. The night of the show, I did feel the sweat bead on my forehead and slide down my temples. But I also did become a performer—at least for one night—with stylized movements, points, vibrating lines. And yes, it does help to imagine your audience naked.

Describe yourself in three words:
Awkward. Imaginative. Searching.

How would someone else describe you?
I get two extremes from people who have just met me: "nice" and "intimidating." The latter may be due to my permanent frown lines. My friend Laura says that I often have a disapproving stare. For most people,

though, I think I'm simply invisible—I'm not a great conversationalist (people are scary, the thought of a phone conversation makes me sweat) and it's not like I'm strikingly beautiful, so I probably leave strangers indifferent. My bosses see me as hard-working and knowledgeable—an out-of-the-box thinker. My coworkers say I'm quiet, which makes for a good listener. Close friends seem to think I'm smart, driven, easily distracted, and a tad self-absorbed. Ask my husband and he'll say that I take pleasure in shocking people (and secretly laughing about it) and that I'm hyperbolic. My grammar school teacher would agree. She once underlined all the adverbs in my essay, ninety-seven. "You need to tone down the drama," she said. My sisters say I complain too much about everything (I'm a perfectionist and a pessimist) and my mom thinks I'm still a child. My dog thinks I'm a canine.

What's your day job?
I teach college writing. Makes me feel relevant.

What do you do for fun?
I'm down for whatever. The movies. The club. The pub. Staying home for a Netflix binge is fine too. Losing myself in books. I recently finished *Santo Vituperio* by my writer-friend Homero Carvalho. I reread Saint Exupéry's *The Little Prince* last night and it brought me to tears.

What's your dream job?
I have it now. I'm teaching writing in Santa Cruz, Bolivia, for one semester. My class meets only twice a week and, because I have six students (instead of the usual thirty), grading isn't tedious. Outside my office hours, I can write, write, and write... sometimes seven hours at a time. My schedule also allows for cultural activities off campus. I get to meet my writer-friends at cafés for espressos and salteñas. We go to concerts and museums and art exhibits. That's how I always imagined the "writing life."

What actors/actresses do you have crushes on?
I don't have crushes on actors. I become obsessed with the *characters* they play. I love smart men: Charlie Eppes (David Krumholtz) in the series *Numbers*, Rancho (Aamir Khan) in the Indian film *Three Idiots*, Neal Caffrey (Matt Bomer) in *White Collar*, and Will (Matt Damon) in *Good Will Hunting*. I am also obsessed with Dr. House (Hugh Laurie). But he is too much of an asshole; my shaky self-esteem would never survive. I don't want to be *with* House. I want to *be* House.

Tell us something your mother doesn't know.
When I was 12, one of the French channels showed porn every night, from 10:00 to 11:00. Having my own TV set, I was able to watch (and dissect) every episode, all the while feasting on peanut butter sandwiches. I rated all the plots, from one to ten. Now I would

probably be an excellent X-rated film critic. (Anyone hiring?) Oh, and Mom? Remember that birthday party at Gaelle's house, in Pèlerin 5? I'm sure you do, because the road's curves are quite memorable. Well, Bernard picked me up minutes after you dropped me off and we went to a club instead.

What advice would you give yourself while going through a bipolar cycle?

Whatever you're thinking right now, it's your brain playing tricks on you. Don't believe a single word. Read a book. Write something.

Where do you want to be in ten years?

I want to have published three American bestsellers. Is that too much to ask the Muse and the Universe?

MARY RAE SMITH
A Hairy Affair

Mary has a BFA from Ohio Wesleyan, an MA and MSW from SUNY Stony Brook, and is an artist, pilot, business consultant and writer from New York City. For more than thirty-five years, Mary has crafted words ranging from sophomoric poetry to grant writing for social causes, with occasional forays into short story fact and fiction. She is a longtime Miami resident and is enchanted by the wonders of life on the ground, in the air and in-between.

A HAIRY AFFAIR
Mary Rae Smith

Four months into chemo, after the last strand of hair drops out, I go on a date.

I haven't dated for twenty years. Not since I was burned by my last "true" love. After that, self-preservation took over. Being mother and provider filled my days. Time passed and I never got back in the game. During these two dry decades, my body went from prom-queen firm to middle-age saggy. And now, I'm also bald.

After two chemo sessions, my *hair* started to hurt. Then it started coming out, so my forty-year-old son offered to shave me. The product of thirteen years in the US Navy, he is not the gentle type. But he is all heart.

I sat in a chair in the middle of the kitchen. He plugged in his electric razor. We drank wine, shaving the edges off reality, until we were ready. Finally, his courage screwed up, he touched the razor to my head.

I cringed and pulled away. "I can't handle it," I said.

My son came up with the solution: He would give me a very short hair cut, not a shave. What hair was left would then fall out when it wanted. No big deal. So simple. And that's what we did.

Now, I'm a bald woman armed with my trusty wig to cover all evil. The wig is as close a match as I could find for the hair I used to have: medium length, brown and wavy. I look in the mirror and think: *See? Nothing's changed. The perfect fit.*

As the chemo takes its course, I tell myself that I live an otherwise normal life. Me and my wig. Others think chemo is so traumatic. The truth about chemo is that you just endure it.

I can handle cancer. But I can't handle being bald. In public, I wear the wig. At home, I wear scarves. I can't even look at myself in the mirror bald. I feel like a thing, totally undesirable, sexless. *Who would even want to look at a bald woman, let alone romance her?*

Then, I meet Carlos in an elevator. He shows interest in me. He asks for my number. He calls. We talk. He asks, "Would you like to go out for dinner?"

I've kept a part of my life at arms length all these years—love, companionship, and intimacy. Now, I've been smacked in the face with my own mortality. Life is fragile. I will take it on, risk a relationship, put myself out there.

I say, "Yes," and, immediately, the doubt creeps in. I have always traded on my looks. What do I do now? Do I tell him about the cancer? The chemo? The wig? Not exactly first-date conversation. But how do I not tell him? And who can I call? What girlfriend can say she has been through this and offer sage advice? It's a lonely vigil.

I envision a myriad of scenarios. In one, I walk the beach with my lover, hand-in-hand, my wig dancing, naturally, in the wind. In another, I tell him about the wig over dinner. He excuses himself to the bathroom and never returns. The one where he accepts me as I am—that one I cannot imagine.

The day arrives before I am ready for it. We go out to dinner, then back to his place for a drink. Then, we are alone, kissing, petting, getting turned on.

"I'm so excited," he whispers. "You're so hot."

We touch, explore and discover each other. He kisses me deeply. He wants me. His hand is underneath my shirt. Mine is lost in his short hair. He kisses my neck. I kiss his face, his cheeks, his eyes. Then he holds me back, looks at me. Looks at my face. I am full of anticipation. He takes my breast, then his hand moves below. I put my hand on him and I feel him grow.

I feel sex—the deep down electricity of sex—for the first time in so long. I am not dead. I am alive.

He lifts my shirt up over my head and drops it to the floor. I lie back on the couch and he presses down on top of me. I close my eyes and lose myself.

In the midst of the kisses and caresses, I open my eyes for a second and look down.

That's when I see it.

The *wig* is on the floor, caught up in the folds of my shirt.

And there I am, in all my romantic glory, bald.

I consider snatching the wig and making a run for the door. But Carlos gracefully ignores my exposure and humiliation. He looks at me again and continues kissing me.

Later, while I dress, I am left with excitement and fear and a renewed sense of hope. Intimacy and love are out there. I am seeking my share.

Q&A WITH MARY
Author of "A Hairy Affair"

How did it feel to tell this story at Lip Service?
Scary at first, vulnerable and ultimately validating.

Describe yourself in three words:
Nice Renaissance woman.

How would someone else describe you in three words?
Smart. Caring. Capable.

What do you do for work?
Business consultant.

What do you do for fun?
Books, movies, travel, new adventures.

What is your dream job?
Painter.

Tell us something your mother doesn't know.
That she was lucky to have two very good kids.

What actors/actresses do you have crushes on?
Christian Bale.

What advice would you give your pre-cancer self?
NEVER SMOKE!!!!!

Where do you want to be in ten years?
In a studio filled with my paintings and the smells and tools of my trade.

That's our book. Thank you for reading. Aquarius. Aquaaaarriiiuuus!

FLIP OVER (THE BOOK)

LIP SERVICE

BADASS

The Double Album

LIP SERVICE

BADASS

The Double Album

Lip Service stories—as good as a kiss.
—Mitchell Kaplan, Books & Books

Delightful, touching, funny, spirited and all true, the stories in Lip Service should be sent up in a satellite or buried in a time capsule. In five hundred years, if anyone is still around to read them, these narratives will be just as entertaining and enlightening as they are now. Lip Service stories are like delicious bonbons—I want more!

—Beverly Donofrio, author of *Riding in Cars with Boys* and *Astonished: A Story of Evil, Blessings, Grace, and Solace*

Eating disorders! Feline overdoses! Star-crossed love! Fist fights! The stories in Lip Service are sharp, funny, and raw. They gave me that lovely shiver I always feel in the presence of beautiful, wrenching truths. Bravo!

—Steve Almond, author of *Candyfreak* and *Against Football*

To everybody who has a story,
which is everybody.

TABLE OF CONTENTS

9   Acknowledgements

11   About the Editor

13   Introduction

21   Sarah Klein
          Obsessed

29   Christina Freedman
          Tar Beach

37   Maureen Fura
          Tied

45   Doug Shear
          Nitro & Glycerin

53   Nicholas Garnett
          Badass

61   Brenda Mezick
          Respect

69   Aaron Curtis
           We Are More Than These Shells

77   Manuel Martinez
           Fake Murder

ACKNOWLEDGEMENTS
Andrea Askowitz

Thank you everybody who had the courage to tell a story at Lip Service and everybody who had the courage to submit a story. And thank you everybody who ever helped Lip Service financially and in-kind, which is a lot of people. Most of these people are listed on our website: **www.lipservicestories.com.**

Thank you, Ellen Ullman, for eyeballing the book and cleaning up our grammar. Thank you, Esther Martinez-Kenniff, for editing these stories for the stage and for always making my stories better. Thank you, Charlotte Howard, who was a joy to work with on the cover, when usually authors and editors barely get a say in what their books look like. Thank you to my entire family for consistently being excited about Lips—my wife, Victoria, who gets as nervous as I get, and especially my brother, Anthony, who told his story from the stage the one time he wasn't Head Usher. Mostly, thank you, M.J. Fievre, who is much more than a publisher. Whenever I thought these stories were ready, M.J. took them apart and put them back together again. Now they're ready.

ANDREA ASKOWITZ
Editor

Andrea tells stories about herself, which is her favorite subject. Her stories have appeared or been heard in places such as the *New York Times*, *Salon.com*, *Jewcy.com*, *Sliver of Stone*, *FourTwoNine*, *NPR*, and *PBS*. She's the author of a memoir, *My Miserable, Lonely, Lesbian Pregnancy*, the creator of Lip Service, and the editor of *Badass*. She grew up in Miami where she lives with her wife, Victoria, and children Natasha, Sebastian, and Beast.

BADASS
LIP SERVICE: TRUE STORIES
THE DOUBLE ALBUM

This is Badass, Lip Service's 8th anniversary debut anthology: The Double Album. We like the number 8[1] at Lip Service since our shows feature 8 storytellers, 8 stories, 8 minutes each. But you got lucky. We decided to create two shows here. So when you're finished with the 8 stories featured on the first A-side, just flip over (the book) and enjoy 8 more.

Thank you for paying for this. If I handed it to you and said, "Ah, don't worry about it," really don't. You could make a donation on our website (**www.lipservicestories.com**) to lessen your guilt, or consider what one of my favorite writing teachers, Joyce Maynard, told a class full of writers: "If you're in this for the money, you might do better getting a job at McDonald's."

I'm Andrea Askowitz, the creator of Lip Service. I'm also the co-producer, co-editor, and co-director of all of our shows, along with Esther Martinez-Kenniff.

---

[1] Okay, grammar lovers, just so you know, we know the rules on how to write numbers. Different style guides give different recommendations. We are using words for any number that can be written with one or two words. But we love the digit 8, so we're breaking the rule. We can; we're badasses.

Lip Service is a true-stories reading series. Every quarter, 8 storytellers tell their stories in front of a live audience.

Before I moved back to Miami 8 years ago, I lived in Los Angeles where there are storytelling events at bars or theaters almost every night of the week. My writer friends and I created Lip Service and hosted a few shows until ours died like so many of them do.

In 2006, I came home. One day, I was sitting in the café at Books & Books talking to a bearded man in black jeans and a blue button down. I told him how I'd organized a storytelling show in Los Angeles and asked him where people in Miami went to tell and hear true stories. Turns out, the man was Mitchell Kaplan, the owner of Books & Books. Mitchell said, "Do it here."

I hung up flyers at a few places around town: Borders Books on U.S. 1 before it closed, the Starbucks on Miracle Mile, Prana Yoga, and the bulletin board on the way to the bathroom at Books & Books. I rallied the students in the writing class I was taking at Borders. I talked to everyone I met. And I solicited thirty-five story submissions. With the help of Goldie Kosow, a seventy-something fireball and one of the writing students in my class, we picked 8 stories, edited them, held a rehearsal, and put together a show.

My mom, a Miami native, leant me her database and I sent emails to my extended family and all three hundred of her friends. There were sixty-five people in our first audience, fifty of them Jewish women in their mid-sixties.

And so, on November 2, 2006, Lip Service was born. Again.

At first I partnered with Goldie Kosow, until she moved to Homestead. Next I partnered with Joe Clifford, an MFA creative writing student and ex-junkie. Joe's first Lip Service submission about a drug trip got rejected because it read like a drug trip. But Joe took it well and submitted another story or two until he got accepted. He was so handsome that, when Goldie moved to Homestead, I asked him to be my Lip Service partner. Joe and I co-produced Lip Service for about two years until he moved to San Francisco where he started, and now produces, Lip Service West.

In November of 2008, Esther Martinez-Kenniff came on board. It was our 8th show. I didn't know Esther before she submitted a story called "Protection" about a bad night with a security guard. The story was sad and honest. Beautiful. She was twenty-nine when she told it at Lip Service, a long way from the seventeen-year-old, mini-skirt-wearing girl in her story.

We've always run Lip Service rehearsals like a writing workshop and, from Esther's first show, I knew that she knew how to edit. She knew how to make stories better. She knew how to get someone else to make his or her story better.

She was so good that, when Joe moved to San Francisco, I asked her to be my Lip Service partner and, in the last six years, Esther and I have taken Lip Service from a free reading at Books & Books (to whom we are forever thankful and still consider our Mac Daddy) to a show that attracts six hundred patrons every time. Two years ago, we won an arts challenge grant from the John S. and James L. Knight Foundation, which is a pretty prestigious prize. We have become a Miami institution.

For every show, Esther and I do more than one hundred hours of work each, which is probably an underestimation. We make money on ticket sales and donations, but our salaries break down to a few dollars an hour. Lip Service is a labor of love.

I think Esther gets the shit work. She thinks I get the shit work. Basically we divide the work based on what we naturally do best. Esther's our banker: She does the accounting, social media, and bill paying. I'm our whore: I do the collaborating, emailing, and money begging. We both do the editing and directing.

We typically do four shows a year on the main stage at Miracle Theater, in Coral Gables. We've also done two Teen Lips and one Spanish Lips (Labios en Español). Once we did a show in Ft. Lauderdale at Cinema Paradiso, once we heated it up for stories about sex by dimming the lights and packing a smaller venue called The Stage, and once we held the Lip Service Olympics as part of Miami's first Lit Crawl. In total, Lip Service has produced thirty-seven shows.

We've also produced Lip Service shows for WLRN, our local National Public Radio station, and WPBT2, our local Public Broadcast Service TV station.

Here's how it works. We send out a call for submissions via email, Facebook and Twitter. Mostly we dredge our local community here, in South Florida, but we accept submissions from anyone in the world. Once a nun from Guatemala flew in to tell a story, so now we call ourselves Lip Service International.

Our storytellers are nuns, lawyers, teachers, FedEx drivers, sports fans, ex-pats, pole-dancers, shower-singers, grandpas, and writers. Everyone has a story.

Sometimes we ask for stories based on a theme—such as "culture clash" or "traffic." Sometimes there's no theme. What we ask for, theme or no theme, is that the stories be true and personal. We don't want true stories about the Revolutionary War. We want true, personal stories in which the storyteller goes through something difficult (often embarrassing) and learns something (usually profound).

If the storyteller tells us the story is true, we believe, since we're a small staff and can't be fact-checking people's lives. Typically we get seventy to eighty story submissions per show. A small secret committee reads all the submissions and picks 8 for the show. Then Esther and I work with each author to get the stories ready for the stage. This process takes three weeks and entails a lot of back and forth (between Esther and me and the authors). There are a lot of discoveries, a lot of revision, a little crying, and sometimes fighting. Sometimes storytellers resist our fine edits.

Then we rehearse. Rehearsal is long and hard, but I love rehearsal because it helps each group become a cohesive cast. When the storytellers tell their stories at rehearsal, some are telling their secrets out loud for the first time. On top of that, we ask them to be open to criticism. Even for someone who's been telling personal stories in front of people for years (me), this moment is terrifying.

Some people sweat. Some talk fast. Some barely speak up. Some cry. Some need a few glasses of wine.

I tell the storytellers that telling a story in front of hundreds of people is a lot easier than telling a story in front of only 8. This is true because with only 8 people in the rehearsal audience, there's very little reaction. And nothing feels worse than telling a story—an act of connecting—to blank stares.

When we get through rehearsal, we are ready. This might sound sappy, but rehearsal always makes me feel like we've created a little family.

You might be one of our audience members. If you are, THANK YOU. You are the best, most supportive, expressive, loving audience in the world. I've told stories all across the country to all different types of people: Jews, queers, old and young people, progressives, conservatives, black people, white people, mixed crowds, (who else is there?) and I've NEVER felt the support of an audience the way I feel it at Lip Service. You have grown from our original audience of sixty-five-year-old Jewish women to a giant mix: six hundred people from all races, religions, creeds, economic backgrounds, and sexual orientations. But while you're a giant mix, you have one thing for sure in common: You share a love of human stories.

Over the last 8 years, you have helped build something miraculous at the Miracle Theater.

A man told the story of connecting with another boy his own age for the first time in the gay section of a video store. When he told us how he reached out and touched the other boy's butt, you gasped. A newlywed told the story about her less-than-perfect honeymoon in Italy. When she told us the abscess on her ass was the size of a ciabatta roll, you laughed like crazy drunks. A scientist told a story about her battle with panic attacks. When her hand trembled on stage, you panicked until she steadied it with her other hand.

The stories are told, but they aren't just listened to. They are experienced.

Every time I walk out of the Miracle Theater after a show, I feel like I've just experienced the musical *Hair*. I want to dance. I want to wave my arms in the air. I want to sing, "Aquarius, Aquaaaarriiiuuus!" I just now figured out why. No one actually takes off his or her clothes on stage, but everyone gets naked.

And that's why I feel so connected. So in love with the storytellers. So in love with the audience. So inspired. Based on what you have told me and based on your recidivism rate, I think you feel it too.

I hope we're able to recreate that feeling here. Enjoy!

Andrea Askowitz
Editor

SARAH KLEIN
Obsessed

Sarah Klein is from small-time Michigan where she was a big-time gymnast. She attended Columbia University and lived in Paris for a year where she milked an obsession with red wine and men with accents. She has a BA, JD, and MBA, and is still trying to figure out what to do with her life. She recently attended the Massachusetts Institute of Technology where she won first place in an entrepreneurship competition. She wants to work for herself so she can kiss her Shih Tzu, Sadie, all day long. She only took to writing stories and airing her family drama on stage a few years ago when she met Andrea Askowitz and Esther Keniff, who encouraged her to say "F*** it" and speak her truth.

OBSESSED
Sarah Klein

My father was obsessed. Obsessed with Paris. Then hot sauces. Then walking sticks. Then hats.

He jumped from obsession to obsession. Just when you'd get used to one, he'd hit you with another. Whatever the thing was, he'd collect it. Talk about it. Buy books on it. Wear it to your school when you asked him not to.

When the obsessions involved clothes or accessories, my mother called them costumes. Like his beekeeper's hat, which was camouflage with a mesh facemask that came down to his shoulders. It had an adjustable elastic drawstring at the bottom of the mesh veil. You could pull it tight to keep bees out or leave it loose to pick your pre-teen daughter up from the Friday night middle school dance.

The beekeeper's hat replaced the Akubra.

"Please don't wear the cowboy hat," my mother pleaded.

"It's not a cowboy hat, it's an *Akubra*. From Australia," my father said. He wore it when he took me to the food court at the mall for lunch at Sbarro. In Lansing, Michigan.

After hats, came cats. We got a cat. And then we got another cat. I got a cat brooch for my birthday. Thirteen-year-olds don't wear brooches and I'd asked for Doc Martens. But for three months, things held steady.

I was just starting to get used to cat-everything when my father woke up one Saturday morning and announced we were going to the store to buy a menorah.

"A what?" I asked.

And just like that, cats became Hanukkah.

We were Catholic. And it was June.

In September, against my mother's wishes, my father enrolled my brother and me in Hebrew school. Because we were the new Jews, the rabbi said we'd have to start at the beginning. So Aaron and I joined the Hebrew school first grade. I was thirteen. Aaron, fourteen.

In the Hebrew school first grade, we colored pictures and sang songs. We ate apples dipped in honey at snack time. I learned the Hebrew alphabet in just two weeks time. In Hebrew school first grade, I shined.

Aaron, however, did not. He wanted to be riding his skateboard or shooting birds with a BB gun in our backyard. He did not want to sing "David Melech Israel" with seven-year-olds.

One Sunday morning, during Hebrew school recess, Aaron locked two of our first-grade classmates in the bathroom with the lights off. They cried and told on him. The rabbi called my father and suggested that

Aaron not return to Hebrew school. Aaron was a bad Jew.

"It's okay," my father reasoned. "I still have one Jewish kid."

The rabbi told my father I was a quick learner and showed signs of Jewish promise. If I continued on this path, he said, I would be promoted to second grade after Hanukkah. My father was overjoyed at this news and hugged me for the first time since I'd bought him a beret. I beamed. I was going to be the best Jew in the world. Top dog. Mispar ekhad.

Around Thanksgiving, I started making my Hanukkah list, which took a lot of time since I had to pick out eight presents instead of the one or two I got when I was Catholic. Even though Aaron wasn't Jewish anymore, he made a list too. Eight was better than one. For this part, he wanted back into the tribe.

In December, I began making careful preparations. I placed a multicolored birthday candle in each of the menorah's nine holes. My father said he didn't think we were supposed to light them all at once—or use birthday candles—but he deferred to me, the resident Jew.

Each night, when he got home from work, he put on the shawl he bought from the Hebrew school gift shop and we played dreidel while our two cats sat on his lap. I sang the Hebrew alphabet and my father clapped along. Aaron ate Doritos.

We were one happy Jewish family.

Except for my mother.

My mother didn't sing or play dreidel. My mother knew that Paris became hot sauces, which became walking sticks, which became hats, which became cats, which became Hanukkah. She knew my father's obsessions had—and would—become our obsessions. Because I would be the best Jew until he fell in love with chamber orchestra music. And then I would be the best violinist until he started collecting tea from around the world. And then I would make a teapot out of clay and give it to him for Father's Day.

The Saturday before Hanukah, my father took us to Thai Kitchen for lunch. Afterward, we went to Bed, Bath & Beyond, where he bought a wok.

I thought nothing of it. But when I got home from school on Monday, I noticed cookbooks lying open on the kitchen counter. *Fast Food Made Asian. 101 Asian Recipes. Mastering the Art of Spring Rolls.*

When Hanukkah arrived just days later, we weren't Jewish anymore. I would never see the Hebrew school second grade, and the menorah was replaced with a Christmas tree. My mom strung the garland and hung stockings. My father cooked wontons.

On Christmas Eve, we went to mass. I sang songs of Hosanna in the Highest and Mary in the manger. And I prayed. I prayed that we would stay on Asian cooking for longer than three months. I prayed that I would be good at it. I prayed that my father would someday make sense to me—that I would someday discover what it was in life I loved; what I liked to do, learn about, collect, read books on.

But mostly, I prayed that Asian cooking would not turn back into hats. My middle school musical was coming up and there was no place in the audience for a beekeeper.

Q&A WITH SARAH
Author of "Obsessed"

How did it feel to tell your story?
Scary. Invigorating. FUN.

What do you do for work?
I'm a full-time law-school administrator. Basically, I'm a life coach for really confused law students. On nights and weekends, I'm a hustler. I am working on starting a business. I would call myself an "entrepreneur" but I haven't actually started anything yet. So I will say that I have an "entrepreneurial spirit" instead. You have to be a little bit crazy to be an entrepreneur so I think I have found my calling.

What do you do for fun?
I learn. I took a poetry class online at Harvard last semester. I read. I smooch my dog. I go to dinner with my mom or with friends. I shop online. I daydream. I play the fiddle and am teaching myself guitar via YouTube.

What is your dream job?
Country music superstar. I don't sing. But I love the big hair and sparkly outfits. I like to consider myself Dolly Parton's biggest fan. As Dolly says, "I'm not offended

by all the dumb blonde jokes because I know I'm not dumb. And I'm not blonde either."

Tell us something your mother doesn't know.
My shattered car window on New Year's Eve was not, actually, a result of vandalism. And the police were not, actually, just giving me a friendly ride home.

What actors/actresses do you have crushes on?
Vince Vaughn. Chelsea Handler.

What advice would you give your thirteen-year-old self?
Work what your mama gave you. Get out of your own way. Braces eventually do come off. Don't waste your time dating Mormons.

Where do you want to be in ten years?
I want to have started and sold my first company. And then my second. And then my third. I want to continue creating things from nothing-but-ideas for the rest of my life. I want to be drinking red wine on the Amalfi Coast and thinking, "Small-town girls from Michigan can make shit happen."

CHRISTINA FREEDMAN
Tar Beach

Growing up in New York City, Christina was always searching for something: the perfect red lipstick, the best song on a mix tape or the peak of the party. At thirty-nine, she bought a one-way ticket to Miami and finally found what she was looking for through writing. Today, Christina lives in South Beach with her husband, Evan, and three Chihuahuas. She is currently working on her memoir.

TAR BEACH
Christina Freedman

It is past noon when you wake up in your childhood bedroom covered in sweat. The chills start first, then hundreds of needles creep up your arms, across the back of your neck, and explode on the top of your head. You reach over for your clothes, left in a pile on the floor, and root around in the pockets for your drugs. There is nothing but an empty wax baggie.

You are out of heroin.

The withdrawal will only get worse. Without money to continue or the stamina to quit, you need to do whatever it takes to feel human again.

This is not the way it was supposed to be. In the 1980s, your mother traded up to a rich boyfriend and a comfortable apartment in Manhattan. She was busy making a living, so you were on your own. Like any young pretty girl, you made the most of it. You had a table at The Odeon and got comped at The Limelight. You thought you were hot shit. In 1990, you graduated from high school and decided you didn't need college. You left to start a new life in Los Angeles, but you never got off the ground. You knew how to look good and collect free drink tickets. Other than that, your skills were limited.

After two years in LA, you were addicted to heroin. You got a restraining order against your junkie boyfriend. When you moved into your car, it got harder to convince yourself that life was great.

You left Los Angeles and crawled back to New York. You begged your mother for forgiveness. She said you couldn't make it without her. Maybe she was right. You promised this time would be different. This time you would stay.

You settled into your old bedroom and kept using.

You were broken down, but you tried to maintain appearances. You wore sugar plum lip-gloss and used concealer to hide your bruises. Your mother became suspicious anyway. She stopped giving you cash. You started stealing from her. At first, you took small things, like the gold locket from her father. Then she caught you walking down Second Avenue with her stereo. That was yesterday.

Today you need to find a way to score.

You put on a blue skirt printed with flowers and a white tank from the suitcase that you never unpacked. You tell yourself that you look passable or at least better than you feel inside. This tiny confidence and some loose change scrounged together gets you on the subway. Every movement is a struggle. A furnace hidden somewhere inside you opens and closes without warning. Your temperature swings wildly. Then, the real pain begins—deep inside your bones.

On the train, you notice people sitting with their belongings unsecured. A purse you could snatch and run with, a chain that could be grabbed from around a frail woman's neck. You remember all the things you would never do before heroin.

You reach your stop. On Clinton Street, you turn left. A dealer named Hector stands in his usual spot on the stoop. Sweat beads on your upper lip. Your mouth waters. You approach Hector, trying to look casual, not desperate.

He motions toward the green metal door of the tenement across the street. He leads you inside. The hall reeks of urine and rotting trash. You follow Hector up the stairs. Acid crawls from your stomach into the back of your throat. You stop on the landing and swallow hard to push it down.

At the top of the stairs, Hector opens a door that leads to the roof.

The tarred roof is hot and black. Metal flecks dot the surface like bits of broken seashells. It reminds you of stories from your mother's childhood. She grew up in a tenement like this one. Her father drank. They never took vacations. Instead, she and her siblings went up to the roof to escape. They pretended they were at the shore. Your mother called it Tar Beach.

Hector hands you a baggie filled with brown powder, worth about twenty dollars. You smile and tell him that you don't have cash today. You hope he'll extend you a credit, like he's done in the past. Hector smiles back. Maybe this will be easy. Then his smile fades and his eyes narrow.

You shove the baggie into your pocket and walk to the door. He grabs your arm and drags you back onto the roof. You look around for help but all you see are the empty windows of distant warehouses. Hector pushes you down on the ground and pins you there. He climbs on top of you and fumbles with his zipper. Sweat seeps through his dirty white T-shirt. He smells of Ballantine Ale and cigarettes.

Hector tears at a condom wrapper with his teeth. You brace yourself.

You close your eyes tight and begin to disappear. You imagine you are on Tar Beach. Hector's heavy breath sounds like the ocean. His motion feels like waves crashing on the shore. Your shame will wash over you and drift out to sea.

The door to the roof swings open. You make out the figure of a man in the doorway. He screams, "Get out of here or I'll call the cops."

Hector leaps up, zips his pants. Your legs are shaking too much to move. Hector offers you his hand and you take it. As you stand, you are wobbly, but it only takes a few seconds for your feet to follow your instincts: You run quickly without looking back. You run away from Hector. You run past the man in the doorway, down the stairs and out onto the sidewalk, all the way to Houston Street. You never stop running.

Your steps only slow when you reach the intersection. Traffic speeds by in both directions. You head north. Adrenaline gives way to dope sickness but now you have the cure. You find a diner and go into the bathroom. In the last stall on the left, you slide the latch shut. You collapse to your knees on the cold tile floor. Sweat runs down your back. Your stomach heaves. You lean over the toilet, but you have nothing left.

    You fall back against the stall and pull a thin strip of aluminum foil from your pocket. You tap the heroin out onto it and fumble for your lighter. You heat the underside of the foil until the powder melts into a pool of black tar. As it bubbles, smoke rises. You inhale deeply.

    The exhale brings instant relief. In this dream world, you don't have hard choices to make. The darkness inside you is lifted. You float off the dirty bathroom floor and up above the grey city streets. You fly so high that, when you look down on the blackened rooftops below, there is no fear of falling.

Q&A WITH CHRISTINA
Author of "Tar Beach"

How did it feel to tell your story?
Electric.

What do you do for work?
Hustle.

What do you do for fun?
I follow TMZ, browse real-estate porn and play with lemurs.

What is your dream job?
Well-kept housewife.

Describe yourself in three words:
A flight risk.

What actors/actresses do you have crushes on?
I've never had a crush.

Tell us something your mother doesn't know.
My address.

What advice would you give your twenty-year-old self?
How to find Evan Freedman's address.

Where do you want to be in ten years?
Wherever life takes me, as long as there's sun.

MAUREEN FURA
Tied

Maureen is the mother of two beautiful, wild boys. She is married to her Captain Nemo, who looks like the god of the sea, Neptune. She is completing her first documentary film, *Dark Side of the Full Moon*, which explores how America is failing mothers. She lives in Coconut Grove and is still a little scared that she bought a house.

TIED
Maureen Fura

I heard you crying down the hall. I knew it was you even though I couldn't see you from my room. You were two days old.

When the nurse rolled your bassinet in, you stopped crying. I like to think it's because you could feel me.

You were a beautiful baby. Not breakable like other newborns. At nine pounds ten ounces, you were the largest baby born in the hospital that week. I named you Soleil, like the sun. You were that for me: life giving and bright.

The night before you were born, Hurricane Bertha was passing through. The pressure in the air pushed heavy until my water broke.

I'd been thinking about who I wanted with us in the delivery room. At first I didn't want her there. This was *my* moment, our last moment. You were still my baby.

But I let her in, your mother, the woman who would adopt you, because I didn't want to disappear with the passage of time. I wanted her to have a complete story to tell you. A story that began with me.

Labor was slow. My body was not ready to let go. Impatient doctors pumped me full of Pitocin. The chemical force squeezed my uterus like soft dough as I clung to the bar on the side of the bed and curled my body into the fetal position. On the monitors, I heard your heart beat. The sound of your heart mixed with my heavy breathing. At the foot of the bed, your mother gently rubbed my feet.

I wasn't always sure I was going to place you for adoption. During the daytime hours I thought you would be mine. But by midnight I would remember I was nineteen and that your father was living 3,000 miles away. *My* child deserved something better than what I could give.

    I received many letters from couples begging for the chance to be your parents but none of them moved me like your mother's. She wrote about family adventures, staying home to raise you, and being able to give you a sister. She was the only one who wrote, "your baby." The only one who promised I would never be erased.

    The first time I met your mother, it was at an Italian restaurant, down the street from my college. I liked her freckles and red hair. She was funny. She looked at me without judgment. She reminded me of my own mother.

    I noticed how she reached for rolls and held her fork. Her hands—their delicate shape, the lack of nail polish. In the hospital bed, all I could think about were those hands. How they comforted me in silence. How they would be the hands that care for you for the rest of your life.

I wished those hands could have been my hands. But my hands weren't good enough. Ready enough.

A week before you were born, I wrote a letter to myself. I wrote it so I would remember what I had to do, afraid that once I saw you I wouldn't be able to let go. I had to remind myself that you deserved a better chance.

When the doctor said it was time to push, I was terrified. I didn't think I was strong enough. I wasn't ready to let go.

As your mother held one leg, and my best friend held the other, I pressed my chin to my chest and pushed. You were so big you couldn't get out. My mother put a mirror in front of me so that I could see you. Your head slid out, and then slipped back in; your shoulders caught on my pelvic bones. Maybe you weren't ready.

The doctor took his knife and cut. I felt the release, your body leaving mine like a cork dislodging from a bottle.

The doctor held you up, and your eyes met mine for the first time. Yours were almond shaped, and dark. For months, I had imagined what you looked like. Once I saw you, I knew it had always been you.

The nurse asked your mother, "Do you want to hold her?"

Your mother said I was supposed to get you first. They lay your wet body on my wobbly stomach and I gazed. You were perfect.

I wanted to give your mother a gift for her promise to give you what I couldn't. I let her cut the cord that tied us.

Three days later I placed you in her arms and watched as the car pulled you away.

Six months later, I was driving on the road close to my school, coming back from class. I was thinking about you. I always thought about you. But this time the feeling was different, as if you were close—somewhere on *that* road. I couldn't shake the feeling. In my mind, I repeated, "My baby is on this road!" as I scanned the passing cars. My heart thumped in my chest.

Then I saw it: your mother's car, the same green minivan you were placed in when you left the hospital. My stomach rolled. I stopped frozen at the wheel and cried. It was you, my baby. I could *still* feel you.

There is an ancient Chinese belief called the red string of fate. According to the belief, special people are tied together for eternity by an invisible red string. Over the past sixteen years, I have thought about you and that moment on the road. I like to think this red string ties us.

Q & A WITH MAUREEN
Author of "Tied"

How did it feel to tell this story?
This was a hard story to tell. It feels like I've been writing it in my head for nineteen years. I gave my birth daughter a copy of the story, which meant the world to me; to let her know she has a beginning. That I was paying attention.

What do you do for work?
Right now, I am a documentary filmmaker on the cusp of finishing my first film on maternal mental-health complications. I like to say I am a social change agent, just finding the right tools to make change.

What do you do for fun?
Take writing classes at Lip Service Institute with Andrea Askowitz. And I have a new addiction to Pinterest.

What is your dream job?
To be the storyteller for the UN.

Describe yourself in three words:
Big laughing momma.

How would someone else describe you?
Silly.

Tell us something your mother doesn't know.
My mom knows everything… except maybe about the drugs.

What advice would you give your nineteen-year-old self?
Girl, you will make it through. I promise. This sucks, but you are brave and strong and your dignity and grace will inspire you one day.

Where do you want to be in ten years?
Ugh. Forty-eight! An accomplished documentary filmmaker, specializing in films about motherhood—exposing, exploring, laughing at, and redefining the oldest job in the world.

DOUG SHEAR
Nitro & Glycerin

Doug is the author of two books: *Rhubarb Culture*, a futuristic novel set in Miami, and *American Karma—Twilight of the Marijuana Gods*, a memoir about hitchhiking across America in the 1970s. His stage play, *Saint Peter at the Gate*, was produced in Toronto, Canada, and Boca Raton, Florida. He writes and performs at various local events, including Life Out Loud, in Ybor City. On rare occasions, Doug performs stand-up comedy at seedy local clubs that he would never visit as a patron.

NITRO & GLYCERIN
Doug Shear

Maria and I didn't start out an interfaith couple. We became one fifteen years into our marriage. Up until then, my wife was a lapsed Catholic and I was a bad Jew. We shared a New Age spirituality and read mystical books to each other as we carpooled to work. We had children and raised them with a schmear of Judaism and a sprinkle of Catholicism.

We weren't interfaith but we were inter-ethnic: Jewish and Cuban, nitro and glycerin. We fell in love the way only opposites fall in love: recklessly, foolishly, and completely.

The truth is I fell in love with Cuban girls a long time ago, when they infiltrated Shenandoah Junior High School. To me they all looked like Gina Lollobrigida, with large breasts, pouty lips, and big, sexy eyes. In spite of our teachers' constant efforts to make them stop, they shook their asses when they walked. The other girls in my class looked like—well—*girls*.

Maria was fascinated by Jewish men. She loved Jewish entertainers like Rodney Dangerfield, Ben Stiller and Sammy Davis Junior. She believed all Jewish men were intelligent and charming, and was surprised to discover I was the exception.

What surprised me about Cubans was the size and complexity of their families. I needed an organizational chart to figure out all of Maria's cousins and uncles and aunts. Throw in the Communist relatives, still in Cuba, and you have the makings of a Latin soap opera: betrayal, deceit, adultery, theft, unpaid loans, even murder.

I had a difficult time remembering who to hate.

And then there were the holidays. Our first Passover took place at my Aunt Ronnie and Uncle Leo's house. Aunt Ronnie greeted us at the door, kissed my cheek, then wet her thumb and smeared the red lipstick.

Maria whispered, "That's disgusting."

As Jews, we had learned to suffer the indignities of slavery, persecution, and overly perfumed mishpocha smearing their saliva on our cheeks. Like my people, I would endure.

Then Aunt Ronnie turned to my wife and said, "Did you know I used to diaper your husband's stinky bottom?"

I said, "Well, not after we got married."

Aunt Ronnie said, "Oh, I diapered him plenty."

"Thanks, Aunt Ronnie. I'll return the favor in a few years."

"He had the cutest little schmeckel," she said, making a tiny space with her thumb and forefinger. "A schmeckel is a penis, dear."

"It grew," I told Aunt Ronnie.

Holidays with Maria's relatives were mucho bueno. I always used a few phrases I learned for the occasion: Feliz Navidad, mucho gusto, pásame la mantequilla por favor. But the phrase I used most is no habla Español. This always elicited disappointment and pity. To make her relatives feel better, I said I understood a lot more Spanish than I spoke. And so I ate my lechón and yuca con mojo and congri— delicious in any language—and pretended to follow the conversation, nodding, laughing, or shaking my head. I'm still not sure what they were talking about, but I think it had to do with my schmeckel.

Then there were the funerals. On the Jewish side, we had weeping women and sobbing men, joke telling, laughing, and lots of food. The more Orthodox Jews, a minority in my family, tore their shirts, gnashed their teeth, and pleaded with the "non-Jews" to fix them plates of food. They insisted the traditional "meal of condolence" must be prepared by friends. My wife and the other non-Jews declined the honor. Eventually, my Orthodox relatives got hungry and made their own heaping plates of condolence and stuffed themselves like, well, not pigs.

The Cuban funerals were always held at the Caballero Rivero Woodlawn Funeral Home. The family joked about buying funeral plots in bulk, and claimed to be on a frequent die-r plan.

Jews don't believe in open caskets, so the first time I saw a dead body was at my wife's cousin's funeral. The deceased, displayed for our viewing pleasure, looked like he was dressed for an interview. Maybe he was. I took my turn stepping up to the coffin.

I wasn't sure what to say. He didn't speak a word of English. I leaned over and whispered, "Feliz Navidad." When Maria took her turn, she walked away sobbing. She explained that her family kept a record of who cried and who didn't, and who dressed like a whore.

In spite of these quirky differences, Maria and I were soul mates. She loved the Jewish holidays, the Jewish food, and the Jewish mother-in-law, and I got to live out my Junior High School fantasies about Cuban girls.

Then, about ten years ago, her soul changed. She became a born-again Christian and we became an interfaith couple.

I didn't think we would make it. We argued about religion night and day. She insisted that Christianity was the only true faith. I accused her of spiritual arrogance. She said, "I'll pray for you."

I considered having an affair with a beautiful co-worker, until my wife told me that, for born-again Christians, the only grounds for divorce was infidelity. Just to get back at her, I didn't cheat.

My wife and I seemed doomed to suffer in a marriage beset by divine differences. Perhaps it was payment for some past-life transgression. Or original sin—depending on which one of us you asked.

According to the Buddhists, every person who comes across our path is a teacher. I began to look at her spirituality as a test. If I could tolerate her spiritual beliefs, but she couldn't tolerate mine, I won!

We began holding each other to a higher standard.

Once, during a fight, I said, "If you're such a saint, how come you screamed at your mother and slammed the phone?"

She said, "If you're so enlightened, how come you didn't tell the cashier she forgot to charge you for the vodka?"

The unintended side effect of all this nonsense was that we both became slightly better people. Over time, we talked about religion less and started to have more fun. As the children got older they made up their own minds about religion.

When we stripped away the brittle layers of theology, Maria and I were soul mates. I thought maybe we would make it after all.

Then Maria became a Republican.

Q&A WITH DOUG
Author of "Nitro & Glycerin"

How did it feel to tell this story?
The story felt kind of sad in the writing, but funny in the telling.

What do you do for work?
I work a lot of different jobs for peanuts, but I've been told I should see it as having multiple income streams. I teach a few marketing classes at a university, do a little marketing for a few clients, sell a little on eBay, and actually figured out how to squeeze a little money out of a few websites I created, like intimatehair.com, primopot.com and moneyslant.com. I don't know. That used to be an easy question.

What do you do for fun?
I grow succulents and desert roses, and sell a few every now and then. One of my multiple income streams.

What is your dream job?
I would love to be a cashier at a Kentucky Fried Chicken. Is there a better job?

Tell us something your mother doesn't know.
Now that question is just too creepy to answer.

What actors/actresses do you have crushes on?
I would leave my wife and family forever for one night with Lucy Lawless.

What advice would you give your pre-married self?
Because of the time-travel paradox I would be afraid to give my pre-married self advice that might end up changing my future for the worse, so I wouldn't say anything. Yeah, I'm that much of a nerd.

Where do you want to be in ten years?
I really don't have any idea. I'm lost.

NICHOLAS GARNETT
Badass

Nicholas received his MFA in creative writing from Florida International University (FIU). He is an adjunct professor at FIU and the Center for Literature and Theatre at Miami Dade College, and the nonfiction editor of *Sliver of Stone*. He is a recipient of residencies from the Vermont Studio Center and the Woodstock Byrdcliffe Guild, and the Norman Mailer Art Colony. Nicholas is the editor of Zimbabwean writer Chenjerai Hove's memoir, *Homeless Sweet Home*. His writing has appeared in *Salon.com*, *Sliver of Stone*, *R-KV-RY Quarterly*, *The Florida Book Review*, *Best of the Net*, *Tigertail, A South Florida Poetry Annual*, *Best Sex Writing of 2013*, and *All That Glitters*, for which he was a contributing editor.

BADASS
Nicholas Garnett

When I was nine, this older kid with a reputation as a badass turned my bare stomach into bongo drums and gave me a pink belly. He had me pinned underneath him, his knees digging into my shoulders. His face was just a few inches above me; he smelled like sweat and cruelty. When the gob of spit dangling from his lips hit me like a water balloon, my anger turned me superhuman. I ended up on top of him, his shoulders pinned under *my* knees. Then, with him just where I wanted him, the anger drained out of me. I shrugged and got up.

That was my last fight. Ever since, I've been known as the nice guy. Sensitive. You get called those things your whole life, you begin to wonder—is nice and sensitive just another way of saying you're a pussy?

A part of me has always wanted to be hard. A badass. Sure, I've done some boxing. But that was exercise, not fighting. There's a difference. Just ask my fiancée, Denise. Now, Denise is a doctor with two kids, but she grew up in the projects in the Bronx with two strikes against her: She was small and she was white. She learned never to back down from anybody, ever. Denise is a badass.

Could I learn to be a badass? It's not about age—Clint Eastwood is still badass at eighty-two—it's about attitude.

Problem is, guys in the suburbs don't get many chances to cop an attitude. Once, I tried using that Clint Eastwood badass squint on a nasty waiter. Denise asked me if I needed new reading glasses. Then, there was that crossing guard who stared me down as I drove past. I thought about pulling over and stepping out of the car—until I remembered I was late picking up Denise's sons from after-care. Plus, I was driving a little red Fiat. A Fiat is about as badass as my little red push mower.

Then, I finally got my chance.

One Saturday night at 3:00 a.m., Denise and I ended up deep in the mean streets of Wilton Manors, at the Courtyard Café. As potential sites to burnish my badass, a gay diner named the Courtyard Café rates pretty low, but as any badass will tell you, "You don't always get to pick your trouble; sometimes trouble picks you."

Trouble took the form of a young drunk guy I named Lippy Lopez. Lippy wore a too-short tank top and a ton of attitude. He staggered over to the booth next to us, stumbled in and dropped his head on the table. Denise went over to make sure he was okay. He raised his head like a cobra and looked at her, cold and hard.

"Hey, chica," he slurred. "Love your hair. I must know—where did you buy it?"

Lippy was intuitive. Denise was overdue getting her extensions redone and had been fretting about her hair for days. She smiled and looked him over, like a fighter looking for a soft spot. Her eyes went to his hairy belly.

She said, "Congratulations. When are you due?"

Lippy said something to Denise in Spanish. Denise shot something back.

Here was where I'd normally diffuse the situation with a joke or a compliment. Not this time. Only one kind of guy lets some lippy sissy insult his woman.

Lippy said, "So, it is old and it speaks Spanish. Like Charro."

Denise laughed. "Let's see what you look like in twenty years, gorda."

A waiter came over to Lippy's table and asked him to leave. He sneered, snatched his car keys and stood up.

He said, "Chica, in twenty years I'll still be fabulous." Lippy looked at me. "And you'll still be looking for a real man."

Just like the time that kid tried to spit in my face, I felt superhuman. I shot up out of my chair.

It was on.

Go time.

It was also time for me to learn some hard lessons about being a badass:

1. Don't ever begin a fight by talking to your opponent like Dirty Harry unless you *are* Dirty Harry.

2. Never place your hands on your opponent's shoulders, unless your strategy is to console your opponent right up until the moment he kicks your ass.

3. If you're not prepared to go all in, don't get in at all. A fight is basically a race to see who makes it first to bat-shit crazy.

4. Don't assume that drunken gay men aren't thoroughly familiar with lessons 1-3.

When Lippy Lopez slashed me across my face with his car keys, I had every reason in the world to go badass. Instead, just like when I was nine, I felt the anger slip out of me. I stood there as the diner transformed itself into an episode of *COPS*. Someone threw a punch at Lippy and hit the waiter. The waiter screamed. The customers screamed.

Denise took one look at the blood streaming down my face and reacted like any forty-something-year-old physician with a couple of kids: She launched herself at Lippy Lopez like a hundred-pound death machine. At the last second, someone caught Denise around her waist and lifted her three feet off the ground. She hovered there, flailing away at the air, a blur of hair and nails and legs and curses. Someone yelled that the police were coming, that we'd all be arrested. We spilled out onto the street. Lippy hightailed it to his car and sped off.

Later that night, I sat on the toilet as Denise patched up my face.

I looked up at her gentle eyes, partially obscured by the ice pack pressed against my nose.

I said, "Some badass, huh?"

She shrugged and said, "You stood up for me. In my book, that's pretty badass."

I guess she was right. Maybe being badass isn't the ability to throw down; it's knowing when to step up.

One thing still gets me, though. It's the thought of Lippy Lopez out there bragging to his friends about what he did to some pussy at the diner.

If I ever see that guy again, I won't be so nice. I'll ask him—no, I'll tell him—to step outside.

Just him and me.

And Denise.

Q&A WITH NICHOLAS
Author of "Badass"

How did it feel to tell this story?
Some of the story was hard to write because it was hard to admit. When I read the story at Lip Service, the most embarrassing parts got the biggest laughs. Now I understand why standup comics are willing to put up with crappy clubs and no money and hecklers. Because when it's all working and you've got the crowd, that shit is *narcotic*. I was buzzing for days. The biggest thing I learned is that one way to be funny is to make fun of yourself.

What do you do for work?
I teach. I edit. I write stuff for and about me and other people.

What do you do for fun?
Bang on drums, lift heavy objects, and admire my wife's ass.

What is your dream job?
To get paid for the stuff I do for free.

Tell us something your mother doesn't know.
How much I miss her.

What actors/actresses do you have crushes on?
Lauren Bacall—for the voice and the attitude. Penelope Cruz—for everything else. If I were inclined to have man-crushes, they'd be on Robert Mitchum and Gerard Butler. I like my men the way I like my women—badasses with brains.

What advice would you give your nine-year-old self?
Punch him, you pussy!

Where do you want to be in ten years?
I grew up in Washington, D.C., then lived in South Beach for ten years. Now, I live in a very nice, quiet suburban community named Cooper City. Did I mention it's quiet? It occurs to me that I've never wanted to live anywhere that has "City" as part of its name: Oklahoma City, Salt Lake City, Atlantic City—they all kind of suck. (I know, there's New York City. But I get around that by calling it Manhattan. Besides, I don't want to live there either.) So, in ten years I'd like to live in a city that doesn't have "City" in its name.

BRENDA MEZICK
Respect

Brenda is a prosecutor and a novelist. She lives in Miami where she collects voodoo dolls.

RESPECT
Brenda Mezick

I'd been an Assistant State Attorney for Miami-Dade County four months when a defense attorney came up to me during court and asked me to spell my full name.

"Is that the exact spelling?" he said, pushing his legal pad in my face. "It has to be exact."

"Why?"

"My client's family wants it."

When he came back and asked for a strand of my hair, I was bewildered. "Absolutely not," I said. But a few moments later, I felt a sharp yank at the back of my head. "Owwww. What the—"

The defense attorney, a licensed member of the Florida Bar, walked the strand of my hair to the defendant's family. I had been violated, but why? A Cuban American prosecutor nearby whispered the word "Santeria." It was all he would say.

Over the years, when I asked other Cubans about Santeria, I got the same tight-lipped reaction. One woman explained, "We might not believe, but we respect."

When I told a fellow prosecutor I thought the little cloth doll placed on his chair during trial was cool, in a slasher film kind of way, he gave it to me. I found another outside the courthouse. I began to collect them, even though they burned my hands a little when I touched them. Then, one evening, after a hearing involving defendants whose families were Santeros, I saw a three-foot, life-like doll, face-up in the gutter outside the courthouse. The detective who was walking me to my office politely ignored what became obvious the closer we got.

It was an effigy of me.

The detective led me away, but I kept looking back at the doll. What do you do if a representation of you has been left lying in a gutter? Do you leave her there where cars could hit her? Do you pick her up? Or would that be like taking home the Bride of Chucky?

I left her, but I wanted answers.

I signed up for a class called Ritualistic Crime Investigation with the City of Miami Police Department. I learned not to pick up those little dolls with my bare hands because they're usually covered in pulverized frog skin or urine.

We went on field trips deep into the heart of Hialeah—to graveyards and botanicas, stores that sell magical items. The first was a combined botanica and "pet store" for "pets" you want to sacrifice. The second botanica specialized in Pahlo, the darkest, most powerful black magic. It looked like an apothecary out of Harry Potter. There were shelves of powders, potions, and dried plants. I came out of that store with a prosecutor's protection kit, complete with beads, potions, and a piece of tree bark that was supposed to heighten my powers of persuasion. I was ready to battle the supernatural.

Two years later, I prosecuted a Pahlo high priest. He was said to have cured cancer and made the lame walk. I charged him with sexual battery. He had molested his stepdaughter from ages six to twelve.

When the child's autistic little sister began obsessively drawing herself being chased by spirits and being lifted to heaven by angels, the family became convinced it was the Pahlo priest sending a warning. They had confidence in me, but they weren't taking chances. They brought in a specialist to dismantle an altar in the priest's backyard. The altar featured an assembly of black cauldrons, where the spirits are housed. The cauldrons were guarded over by life-size statues. Siete Rayos, the deity of war, wielded an action-figure sword—the same sword the child had watched the Pahlo priest hold to her mother's throat.

When the child testified by closed-circuit TV, strange things happened. First there were technical difficulties with the closed-circuit system. When we got reception, the child froze in fear and wouldn't answer my questions. Then, when she finally started talking, an electrical power surge raised the clerk's table and the judge's bench off the floor like a wave. One of the jurors gave me a look, like, "No way." I turned to the Pahlo priest. He smiled.

Now, he's doing a life sentence.

I'm not sure if the protective powder I dabbed behind my ears or the bark I chewed that morning had any effect on the outcome of the trial. But even if I don't believe, I too have learned to respect.

Q&A WITH BRENDA
Author of "Respect"

How did it feel to tell this story?
I was a little nervous about the reactions I would get at the office, but they took it well.

Describe yourself in five words.
Perspicacious. Direct. Intuitive. Bibliophile. Evolving.

How would someone else describe you in five words?
I asked a few people and liked these best: tenacious, deep, intriguing, luminous, and dynamic.

What do you do for work?
Prosecutor.

What do you do for fun?
Read, write and sign up for yoga classes on Groupon.

What is your dream job?
To be a commercially successful novelist.

Tell us something your mother doesn't know.
No.

What actors/actresses do you have crushes on?
I don't have crushes on actors, but I do have crushes on characters as played by certain actors. Big crush on Dyson in *Lost Girl* played by Kris Holden-Reid. Even bigger crush on Daryl Dixon played by Norman Reedus in *The Walking Dead*.

What advice would you give your high-school self?
"Don't marry that guy."

Where do you want to be in ten years?
Writing in a cottage by the sea with my soul mate, who preferably has a very sexy Irish accent and a lot of patience.

AARON CURTIS
We Are More than These Shells

Born in Syracuse, NY, Aaron moved to Miami in 1997. He had a monthly column called "Book Junky" in the now defunct *Moxxi Magazine*, he wrote poetry and short stories on tap for MANO Fine Art's "Borrowed Words" exhibition in April 2014, and his essay "It Grows on You" appeared in the *World Book Night 2014* ebook. You can find him online at Sweet with Fall and Fish.

WE ARE MORE THAN THESE SHELLS
Aaron Curtis

I met Kelly while selling tickets for a dance during my sophomore year of high school. Dressed in bulky, long-sleeved layers despite the eighty-degree weather, Kelly stood out. She had black hair in loose curls, dark brown eyes, pale skin with high color on her cheeks, and perfect bow lips: Snow White in wire-framed glasses.

Anorexia and bulimia were just becoming part of the national consciousness. One look at Kelly's five-foot seven, ninety-pound frame and I assumed I'd met my first real-life sufferer. Then she spoke. Kelly sounded like a willow tree, delicate-looking but impossible to topple.

She bought two tickets for the winter cotillion. She was leaning on crutches and joked about being off of them by December. She smiled easily, and with genuine joy.

I didn't know it at the time, but the crutches were due to her third broken hip. Kelly had been born months premature, less than two pounds of struggling baby-bird tissue in an incubator. Doctors told her parents Kelly wouldn't last the night. When Kelly lasted the night, her doctors called it a miracle. They told Kelly's parents she wouldn't last a week.

Thus the map of Kelly's life was drawn. Doctors set deadlines they called impossible, and Kelly proved them wrong. Over the years, Kelly's doctors advised her parents to make funeral arrangements so often it became a joke. Kelly was seventeen when we met. She had been battling cystic fibrosis her entire life.

Two things about her illness bothered her. She had a port in her chest for needles and IVs—what she called her third nipple—and the tips of her long, delicate fingers were slightly bulbous. Birdie hands, she called them. Apart from complaining about those things from time to time, she was the most optimistic person I had ever met.

More than anything, Kelly loved to laugh. I'd push jokes until she screamed, her voice losing air until she dissolved into a coughing fit, leaving her red-faced, tears running from her eyes. It sounds terrible, but it was an ecstatic loss of control. She said those laughing jags were worth the coughing fits.

In contrast to Kelly, I spent most days miserable, snapping at people closest to me, taking umbrage at every minor inconvenience, punching my knuckles bruised and bloody on the concrete floor of my parents' basement to relieve some of the pain inside.

"God, you're such as asshole," Kelly told me once. I can't remember what I said to provoke it but I remember she wasn't joking. "Can't you just be happy?"

No, I couldn't. My misery was hormonal, worn like an uncomfortable coat in rough weather.

A few weeks after I sold Kelly tickets, I began dating her best friend. Kelly watched my two-year relationship with Micky unfold. Micky and I fought almost constantly, if you can call my passive-aggressive silent brooding "fighting." She knew Micky took my virginity and the lead in all things sexual. She knew Micky became pregnant in our second year. She knew Micky got an abortion, broke up with me, and started college, leaving me behind in high school.

That summer, Kelly and I went to see Edie Brickell and the New Bohemians in concert. Even though Kelly had graduated high school, she confessed a crush on someone who'd be starting his senior year in the fall. Playing the girlfriend role, I giggled over the details.

"He's tall, with black hair and brown eyes," she said.

I threw out some names, but she shook her head.

"His initials are A.C."

"Allen Clark," I said immediately.

"No." She turned from the stage, looking up at me hopefully.

"Well, Art Constanza isn't really tall..."

"No..."

"And Alan Carter's going to be a junior..."

"Yeah..."

Finally, I realized who she meant. And panicked.

Kelly had told Micky one of her biggest fears was dying a virgin. I couldn't face that kind of pressure, being someone's first, last, and only.

Kelly had also briefly dated *my* best friend. In the manner of adolescent boys, he had described her body in some detail. The small torso, the ribs pressing against her skinny flesh, her lack of any breast tissue, the shelf of her pelvic bone. Despite her height, and as pretty as Kelly's face was, I would have felt like a pedophile. I didn't have the emotional capacity to look past the flesh at the soul beneath, the soul I loved.

Or maybe I was just scared to grow closer to someone who I knew could leave at any moment. The doctors had marked age twenty as the new impossible milestone. Kelly joked that this time they meant it.

Of course, I articulated none of this. Standing beside her at the concert, I went silent. I stared at the stage while Kelly watched me in the dark. She knew my patterns by then, and got the message before too long.

"Nevermind," she said, turning to the stage. "Forget it, there's no one."

My callous reaction was immature, regrettable, and impossible to forget. Our relationship never recovered, and we drifted apart. She died shortly after, at nineteen years old. She had started college. Her boyfriend was a junior in high school, a dark-haired stutterer with whom Kelly and I had shared a drama class. I wondered if he'd taken her virginity but didn't have the guts or the gall to ask.

In the casket, I expected her to be emaciated. Instead, steroids had bloated her torso and distorted her pretty face. Regret over how our friendship ended mixed with my grief. The tear-streaked faces of her family and our friends became accusations, like they knew I was guilty of abandoning her when she most needed me.

I'm nearly twice as old as I was when I looked into that casket. I wish I could say that I always look on the bright side of life because of Kelly, but it's a lesson I relearn often.

My wife and I met in college. She was diagnosed with IgA nephropathy at age twenty-four, rejected a kidney transplant at twenty-six, and has been on dialysis for ten years. In her complaints over the myriad ways the disease has affected her body, I hear the ghost of my childhood friend. Now I don't pull away. I offer assurances that she is more beautiful today than the day we met, which is nothing but the absolute truth. She accuses me of wearing love goggles.

If that's the case, I have Kelly to thank for showing me their importance.

Q&A WITH AARON
Author of "We Are More Than These Shells"

How did it feel to tell this story?
Vulnerable. Making a heroically-suffering, tragically-afflicted young woman feel bad about herself is not my finest moment as a human being. It's also frustrating because I could never capture how amazing she was. Coping with cystic fibrosis stole her childhood and made a normal life impossible, but she always had a smile on her face and made everyone around her smile too.

What do you do for work?
Since 2004, I've worked at South Florida's largest independent bookstore, Books & Books.

What do you do for fun?
Read, blog, watch movies. Binge-watch TV shows on Netflix then get sad when they're over. I love cooking and even have a red ribbon from the Dade County Youth Fair for my Harvest Chili.

What is your dream job?
Books & Books is a great place to be. I'd be there part time, and writing would cover the rest. Wow, that's. . . realistic. In dreamland, my screenplay wins an Oscar and I end up running a show for HBO.

Tell us something your mother doesn't know.
That when you text someone, you don't need to put your name on it.

What actors/actresses do you have crushes on?
I reject this question because crushes are painful, giddy things that only happen with people you know. Also, Eva Mendes.

What advice would you give your high school self?
It gets better, wear a condom, see *Miller's Crossing* and not *The Adventures of Ford Fairlane*, the popular kid's opinions won't mean anything ten minutes after graduation, don't cut your own hair with dad's electric shaver, and join drama club instead of football. Oh, and all that acid you're going to do in a few years? Maybe, you know, not so much.

Where do you want to be in ten years?
New Orleans.

MANUEL MARTINEZ
Fake Murder

Manuel (Manny) grew up in Miami, and attended the University of Florida where he received his MFA in fiction. His stories have appeared in a number of publications including *The Quarterly*, *Bridge*, *The Sun*, and *Hotel Amerika*. He lives in Brooklyn, where his apartment is too small for him to store more than one cooler. He is therefore not prepared for any situation requiring large amounts of beverages.

FAKE MURDER
Manuel Martinez

While I was lying face down in the grass, pretending to have just been shot, I realized the extent to which my friends and I had not thought this whole thing through.

The lawn was exquisitely manicured and sat on a quiet street in Miami Shores. This is where the Pope stayed when he visited Miami. It is not a neighborhood where, on a quiet Saturday afternoon, anyone expects to see a black teenager in handcuffs jump out of a car, run across someone's front yard, and then get shot three times before collapsing in the grass.

Such a stunt was not unprecedented for me and my friends. They were brothers who lived in Miami Shores. We spent our time making small bombs and attacking our enemies' cars and houses with eggs and BB guns. We liked to take things that weren't ours, not only the starting pistol we'd borrowed from the office of our high school track coach and used to shoot me, but also sodium from the chemistry lab, which ignites upon contact with water and is therefore quite spectacular when thrown into someone's pool. We cruised Coral Gables and Key Biscayne at night, looking for landscaped yards where the staghorns and palms were lit with floodlights that we would steal for our band's light show. We stole anything we could get away with, and when our parents asked where any of these things had come from, my friends and I would say, "We've had that for a long time."

We were never ones to think carefully about the consequences of our actions, which is why we decided that it would be a good idea for me to put on a pair of trick handcuffs and run into someone's yard, while one of my friends pretended to shoot me with a starting pistol.

When the shots were fired, my friends screeched away in their mother's car and I fell down in the grass, prepared to stay all day if that's what it took to make this look real. That was my biggest concern at the time, that witnesses actually be fooled into thinking they had seen a drug deal go bad in their safe and quiet neighborhood. But we hadn't thought far enough ahead to consider how we would make a realistic getaway and whether I was supposed to be either dead or incapacitated.

When one of my friends ran across the lawn and knelt down to whisper in my ear, "Get in the car, this isn't going well," I did as he said but was overcome with disappointment because surely no one would believe that the shootee in such a situation would run back into the car of the shooter simply because of a few whispered words.

We drove back to my friends' house a few blocks away, and their parents could tell something was wrong, but they had learned not to pry too much into our activities and left us alone to commiserate over our failed plan. Fifteen minutes later, when we were sure that the whole thing had blown over, we headed out again. We were only a block away when a police car pulled us over. The officer came over to my side, the passenger side of the car, and leaned down into my open window.

"What you boys been up to today?" he asked.

"Just driving around," I said.

"Just driving around," he repeated, then looked at me, at my afro that was much too large to be fashionable in 1984, and said, "You've got some grass in your hair. You been rolling around in the grass?"

"We were wrestling in the front yard," I said.

He then matter-of-factly asked, "You boys pull a little stunt earlier about somebody getting shot?"

He asked so disarmingly, so casually that we responded in unison with, "Yeah, that was us," and he told us to wait while he went back to his car, and given the casual tone, I expected he would come back, tell us not to fake any murders in the future, and send us on our way.

Instead, within five minutes, there were nine police cars surrounding us, with a total of thirteen cops representing Miami Shores, Metro-Dade, and the SWAT team, and each cop felt it was his right and duty to yell at each of us, and through all this yelling we learned that an APB had been put out on us from Key West to the Broward County line; that we had been designated armed and dangerous, which meant that had we made any strange moves during our apprehension we would have been shot; that a helicopter had been dispatched to search for us; and that all of this had cost the city (somehow they had the figures ready) twenty-thousand dollars, which we might have to repay.

We were then handcuffed for real, placed in the back of a patrol car, and carted away to the Miami Shores police station and jail. We were put in two cells down the hall from some offices that were conspicuously lacking any of the grit of the police stations on television, and since the older of the brothers was eighteen and technically an adult, he was put into one cell by himself to keep him from corrupting his brother and me.

We very quickly picked up on the basics of prison communication, though, and began talking through the air ducts, and my cellmate and I, feeling that the pain of incarceration could only be eased by song, sang "Swing Low Sweet Chariot" and other spirituals to our comrade in isolation.

After an hour or so, we were called into a room that looked like a principal's office.

The chief, or whoever it was behind the desk, some guy in a tie who had to work hard to look stern, pointed at my eighteen-year-old friend and said, "We could arrest you for contributing to the delinquency of a minor."

My friend began to nod obsequiously, while his brother and I had to stifle our laughter. We knew we wouldn't be charged with anything, that we would have to sit through a lecture complete with finger pointing, empty threats and admonishments to not think this was funny, after which we would be released to our parents who would lecture and threaten and warn us again.

I tell this story every so often, at bars and parties, and the older I get, the further I get from the events themselves, the more I can convince myself that the experience taught me to be more cautious, that it taught me to plan and to think things through. But in reality, I long for the time when I was so adrift, when I was face down in the lawn, unaware of what was going to happen next.

Q&A WITH MANUEL
Author of "Fake Murder"

How did it feel to tell this story at Lip Service?
It was wonderfully surprising to hear people laugh.

What do you do for work?
I teach freshman composition and literature.

What do you do for fun?
I try to get on or under the water as much as I possibly can.

What is your dream job?
To write every morning and run errands every afternoon.

Describe yourself in three words:
Impatient. Sloppy. Confused.

How would someone else describe you?
Confused.

Tell us something your mother doesn't know.
I used to skip church.

What actors/actresses do you have crushes on?
Maura Tierney, Jennifer Jason Leigh.

What advice would you give your seventeen-year-old self?
Go off on your own.

Where do you want to be in ten years?
Some place I've never been before.